KU-715-783

B.C.H.E. - LIBRARY
00158705

The Accursed Share

Volume I

Translated by Robert Hurley

The Accursed Share

Volume I

The Accursed Share

An Essay on General Economy

Georges Bataille

Volume I

Consumption

ZONE BOOKS · NEW YORK

1991

BATH COLLEGE OF HIGHER EDUCATION
DISCARD
LIBRARY
8 SOMERSET PLACE,
BATH. BA1 5HB.

330
BAT

© 1988 Urzone, Inc.
ZONE BOOKS
611 Broadway Suite 838
New York, NY 10012

First Paperback Edition

All rights reserved

No part of this book may be reproduced, stored in a
retrieval system, or transmitted in any form or by
any means, including electronic, mechanical, photo-
copying, microfilming, recording, or otherwise (except
for that copying permitted by Sections 107 and 108
of the U.S. Copyright Law and except by reviewers for
the public press) without written permission from
the Publisher

Originally published in France as *La Part Maudite*
© 1967 by Les Éditions de Minuit.

Printed in the United States of America

Distributed by The MIT Press,
Cambridge, Massachusetts, and London, England

Library of Congress Cataloging-in-Publication Data

Bataille, Georges, 1897-1962.
    The accursed share.

    Translation of: La part maudite.
    Bibliography: p.
    1. Economics. I. Title.
HB173.B35513 1988   330   87-34072
ISBN 0-942299-10-8
ISBN 0-942299-11-6 (pbk.)

Exuberance is beauty.
WILLIAM BLAKE

Contents

Preface

For some years, being obliged on occasion to answer the question "What are you working on?" I was embarrassed to have to say, "A book of political economy." Coming from me, this venture was disconcerting, at least to those who did not know me well. (The interest that is usually conferred on my books is of a literary sort and this was doubtless to be expected: One cannot as a matter of fact class them in a pre-defined genre.) I am still annoyed when I recall the superficial astonishment that greeted my reply; I had to explain myself, and what I was able to say in a few words was neither precise nor intelligible. Indeed, I had to add that the book I was writing (which I am now publishing) did not consider the facts the way qualified economists do, that I had a point of view from which a human sacrifice, the construction of a church or the gift of a jewel were no less interesting than the sale of wheat. In short, I had to try in vain to make clear the notion of a "general economy" in which the "expenditure" (the "consumption") of wealth, rather than production, was the primary object. My difficulty increased if I was asked the book's title. *The Accursed Share*: It might be intriguing, but it wasn't informative. Yet I should have gone further, then, and affirmed the desire to lift the curse that this title calls into question. Clearly, my project was too vast and

9

the announcement of a vast project is always its betrayal. No one can say without being comical that he is getting ready to overturn things: He must overturn, and that is all.

Today the book is there. But a book is nothing if it is not *situated*, if criticism has not determined the place that belongs to it in the common movement of ideas. Again, I find myself faced with the same difficulty. The book is there, but at the moment of writing its preface I cannot even ask that it be given the attention of specialists in a science. This first essay addresses, from outside the separate disciplines, a problem that still has not been framed as it should be, one that may hold the key to all the problems posed by every discipline concerned with the movement of energy on the earth – from geophysics to political economy, by way of sociology, history and biology. Moreover, neither psychology nor, in general, philosophy can be considered free of this primary question of economy. Even what may be said of art, of literature, of poetry has an essential connection with the movement I study: that of excess energy, translated into the effervescence of life. The result is that such a book, being of interest to everyone, could well be of interest to no one.

Certainly, it is dangerous, in extending the frigid research of the sciences, to come to a point where one's object no longer leaves one unaffected, where, on the contrary, it is what inflames. Indeed, the ebullition I consider, which animates the globe, is also *my* ebullition. Thus, the object of my research cannot be distinguished *from the subject at its boiling point*. In this way, even before finding a difficulty in receiving its place in the common movement of ideas, my enterprise came up against the most personal obstacle, which moreover gives the book its fundamental meaning.

As I considered the object of my study, I could not personally resist the effervescence in which I discovered the unavoidable purpose, the value of the cold and calculated operation. My research aimed at the acquisition of a knowledge; it demanded coldness and calculation, but the knowledge acquired was that of an error, an error implied in the coldness that is inherent in all calculation. In other words, my work tended first of all to *increase* the sum of human resources, but its findings showed me that this accumulation was only a delay, a shrinking back from the inevitable term, where the accumulated wealth has value only in the instant. Writing this book in which I was saying that energy finally can only be wasted, I myself was using my energy, my time, working; my research answered in a fundamental way the desire to add to the amount of wealth acquired for mankind. Should I say that under these conditions I sometimes could only respond to the truth of my book and could not go on writing it?

A book that no one awaits, that answers no formulated question, that the author would not have written if he had followed its lesson to the letter — such is finally the oddity that today I offer the reader. This invites distrust at the outset, *and yet*, what if it were better not to meet any expectation and to offer precisely that which repels, that which people deliberately avoid, for lack of strength: that violent movement, sudden and shocking, which jostles the mind, taking away its tranquillity; a kind of bold reversal that substitutes a dynamism, in harmony with the world, for the stagnation of isolated ideas, of stubborn problems born of an anxiety that refused to *see*. How, without turning my back on expectations, could I have had the extreme freedom of thought that places concepts on a level with the world's freedom of movement? It would serve no purpose to neglect the rules of rigorous investigation, which proceeds slowly and methodically. But how can we solve the enigma, how can we measure up to the universe if we content ourselves with the slumber of conventional knowledge? If one has the patience, and the courage, to read my book, one will see that it contains studies conducted according to the rules of a reason that does not relent, and solutions to political problems deriving from a traditional wisdom, but one will also find in it this affirmation: *that the sexual act is in time what the tiger is in space.* The comparison follows from considerations of energy economy that leave no room for poetic fantasy, but it requires thinking on a level with a play of forces that runs counter to ordinary calculations, a play of forces based on the laws that govern us. In short, the perspectives where such truths appear are those in which more general propositions reveal their meaning, propositions according to which *it is not necessity but its contrary, "luxury," that presents living matter and mankind with their fundamental problems.*

This being said, I will urge critics to be somewhat cautious. It is an easy game to raise irrefutable objections to new views. Generally, that which is new is disconcerting and not correctly understood: The objections are directed at simplified aspects that the author does not grant any more than a would-be contradictor, or grants only within the limits of a provisional simplification. There is little chance in the present case that these peremptory difficulties, which stand out at the first reading, have escaped my attention in the 18 years this work has demanded of me. But, to begin with, I confine myself to a quick overview, in which I cannot even consider broaching the multitude of questions that are implied.

In particular, I have foregone the idea of giving, in a first volume, a detailed analysis of all of life's actions from the point of view that I introduce. This is regrettable in that the notions of "productive expenditure" and "nonproductive expenditure" have a basic value in all the developments of my book. But real life, composed of all sorts of expenditures, knows nothing of purely productive expenditure; in actuality, it knows nothing of purely nonproductive expenditure either. Hence a first rudimentary classification will have to be replaced by a methodical description of every aspect of life. I wanted first to offer a group of privileged facts that would allow my thinking to be grasped. But this thinking could not have shaped itself if it had not also considered the totality of small occurrences, wrongly supposed to be insignificant.

I imagine that it would be equally futile to draw destructive conclusions from the fact that economic crises, which necessarily have in my work a sense in which they are decisive events, are only represented therein in a summary, superficial fashion. If the truth must be told, I had to choose: I could not at the same time give my thinking a general outline, and lose myself in a maze of interferences, where the trees constantly prevent one from seeing the forest. I wanted to avoid redoing the work of the economists, and I confined myself to relating the problem that is posed in economic crises to the general problem of nature. I wanted to cast a new light on it, but to start with, I decided against analyzing the complexities of a crisis of overproduction, just as I deferred calculating in detail the share of growth and the share of waste entering into the manufacture of a hat or a chair. I preferred to give, in general, the reasons that account for the mystery of Keynes's bottles, tracing the exhausting detours of exuberance through eating, death and sexual reproduction.

I confine myself at present to this summary view. This does not mean that I am leaving it at that: I am only postponing more extensive work until later.[1] I am also postponing, for a short time, the exposition of my analysis of anxiety.

And yet that is the crucial analysis that alone can adequately circumscribe the opposition of two political methods: that of fear and the anxious search for a solution, combining the pursuit of freedom with the imperatives that are the most opposed to freedom; and that of freedom of mind, which issues from the global resources of life, a freedom for which, instantly, everything is resolved, *everything is rich* — in other words, everything that is commensurate with the universe. I insist on the fact that, to freedom of mind, the search for a solution is an exuberance, a superfluity; this gives it an incomparable force. To solve political problems becomes difficult for those who allow anxiety alone to pose them. It is necessary for anxiety to pose them. But their solution demands at a certain point the removal of this anxiety. The meaning of the political proposals to which this book leads, and that I formulate at the end of the volume, is linked to this lucid attitude.[2]

PART ONE

Theoretical Introduction

The Meaning of General Economy

The Dependence of the Economy on the Circulation of Energy on the Earth

When it is necessary to change an automobile tire, open an abcess or plow a vineyard, it is easy to manage a quite limited operation. The elements on which the action is brought to bear are not completely isolated from the rest of the world, but it is possible to act on them as if they were: One can complete the operation without once needing to consider the whole, of which the tire, the abcess or the vineyard is nevertheless an integral part. The changes brought about do not perceptibly alter the other things, nor does the ceaseless action from without have an appreciable effect on the conduct of the operation. But things are different when we consider a substantial economic activity such as the production of automobiles in the United States, or, *a fortiori*, when it is a question of economic activity in general.

Between the production of automobiles and the *general* movement of the economy, the interdependence is rather clear, but the economy taken as a whole is usually studied as if it were a matter of an isolatable system of operation. Production and consumption are linked together, but, considered jointly, it does not seem difficult to study them as one might study an elementary operation relatively independent of that which it is not.

19

This method is legitimate, and science never proceeds differently. However, economic science does not give results of the same order as physics studying, first, a precise phenomenon, then all studiable phenomena as a coordinated whole. Economic phenomena are not easy to isolate, and their general coordination is not easy to establish. So it is possible to raise this question concerning them: Shouldn't productive activity as a whole be considered in terms of the modifications it receives from its surroundings or brings about in its surroundings? In other words, isn't there a need to study the system of human production and consumption within a much larger framework?

In the sciences such problems ordinarily have an academic character, but economic activity is so far-reaching that no one will be surprised if a first question is followed by other, less abstract ones: In overall industrial development, are there not social conflicts and planetary wars? In the global activity of men, in short, are there not causes and effects that will appear only provided that *the general data of the economy* are studied? Will we be able to make ourselves the masters of such a dangerous activity (and one that we could not abandon in any case) without having grasped its *general* consequences? Should we not, given the constant development of economic forces, pose the *general* problems that are linked to the movement of energy on the globe?

These questions allow one to glimpse both the theoretical meaning and the practical importance of the principles they introduce.

The Necessity of Losing the Excess Energy that Cannot be Used for a System's Growth

At first sight, it is easy to recognize in the economy — *in the production and use of wealth* — a particular aspect of terrestrial activity regarded as a cosmic phenomenon. A movement is produced on the surface of the globe that results from the circulation of energy at this point in the universe. The economic activity of men appropriates this movement, making use of the resulting possibilities for certain ends. But this movement has a pattern and laws with which, as a rule, those who use them and depend on them are unacquainted. Thus the question arises: Is the general determination of energy circulating in the biosphere altered by man's activity? Or rather, isn't the latter's intention vitiated by a determination of which it is ignorant, which it overlooks and cannot change?

Without waiting, I will give an inescapable answer.

Man's disregard for the material basis of his life still causes him to err in a serious way. Humanity exploits given material resources, but by restricting them as it does to a resolution of the immediate difficulties it encounters (a resolution which it has hastily had to define as an ideal), it assigns to the forces it employs an end which they cannot have. Beyond our immediate ends, man's activity in fact pursues the useless and infinite fulfillment of the universe.[1]

Of course, the error that results from so complete a disregard does not just concern man's claim to lucidity. It is not easy to realize one's own ends if one must, in trying to do so, carry out a movement that surpasses them. No doubt these ends and this movement may not be entirely irreconcilable; but if these two terms are to be reconciled we must cease to ignore one of them; otherwise, our works quickly turn to catastrophe.

I will begin with a basic fact: The living organism, in a situation determined by the play of energy on the surface of the globe, ordinarily receives more energy than is necessary for maintaining life; the excess energy (wealth) can be used for the growth of a system (e.g., an organism); if the system can no longer grow, or if the excess cannot be completely absorbed in its growth, it must necessarily be lost without profit; it must be spent, willingly or not, gloriously or catastrophically.

The Poverty of Organisms or Limited Systems and the Excess Wealth of Living Nature

Minds accustomed to seeing the development of productive forces as the ideal end of activity refuse to recognize that energy, which constitutes wealth, must ultimately be spent lavishly (without return), and that a series of profitable operations has absolutely no other effect than the squandering of profits. To affirm that it is necessary to dissipate a substantial portion of energy produced, sending it up in smoke, is to go against judgments that form the basis of a rational economy. We know cases where wealth has had to be destroyed (coffee thrown into the sea), but these scandals cannot reasonably be offered as examples to follow. They are the acknowledgment of an impotence, and no one could find in them the image and essence of wealth. Indeed, involuntary destruction (such as the disposal of coffee overboard) has in every case the meaning of failure; it is experienced as a misfortune; in no way can it be presented as desirable. And yet it is the type of operation without which there is no solution. When one considers the *totality* of productive wealth on the surface of the globe, it is evident that the products of this wealth can be employed for productive ends only insofar as the living organism that is economic mankind can increase its equipment. This is not entirely — neither always nor indefinitely — possible. A surplus must be dissipated through deficit operations: The final dissipation cannot fail to carry out the movement that animates terrestrial energy.

The contrary usually appears for the reason that the economy is never considered *in general*. The human mind reduces operations, in science as in life, to an entity based on typical *particular* systems (organisms or enterprises). Economic activity, considered as a whole, is conceived in terms of particular operations with limited ends. The mind generalizes by composing the aggregate

22

of these operations. Economic science merely generalizes the isolated situation; it restricts its object to operations carried out with
a view to a limited end, that of economic man. It does not take
into consideration a play of energy that no particular end limits:
the play of *living matter in general*, involved in the movement of
light of which it is the result. On the surface of the globe, for
living matter in general, energy is always in excess; the question is
always posed in terms of extravagance. The choice is limited to
how the wealth is to be squandered. It is to the *particular* living
being, or to limited populations of living beings, that the problem of necessity presents itself. But man is not just the separate
being that contends with the living world and with other men
for his share of resources. The general movement of exudation
(of waste) of living matter impels him, and he cannot stop it; moreover, being at the summit, his sovereignty in the living world iden-
tifies him with this movement; it destines him, in a privileged
way, to that glorious operation, to useless consumption. If he
denies this, as he is constantly urged to do by the consciousness
of a *necessity*, of an indigence inherent in separate beings (which
are constantly short of resources, which are nothing but eternally
needy individuals), his denial does not alter the global movement
of energy in the least: The latter cannot accumulate limitlessly
in the productive forces; eventually, like a river into the sea, it is
bound to escape us and be lost to us.

War Considered as a Catastrophic Expenditure
of Excess Energy

Incomprehension does not change the final outcome in the slight-
est. We can ignore or forget the fact that the ground we live on
is little other than a field of multiple destructions. Our ignorance
only has this incontestable effect: It causes us to *undergo* what we
could *bring about* in our own way, if we understood. It deprives

us of the choice of an exudation that might suit us. Above all, it consigns men and their works to catastrophic destructions. For if we do not have the force to destroy the surplus energy ourselves, it cannot be used, and, like an unbroken animal that cannot be trained, it is this energy that destroys us; it is we who pay the price of the inevitable explosion.

These excesses of life force, which locally block the poorest economies, are in fact the most dangerous factors of ruination. Hence relieving the blockage was always, if only in the darkest region of consciousness, the object of a feverish pursuit. Ancient societies found relief in festivals; some erected admirable monuments that had no useful purpose; we use the excess to multiply "services" that make life smoother,[2] and we are led to reabsorb part of it by increasing leisure time. But these diversions have always been inadequate: Their existence *in excess* nevertheless (in certain respects) has perpetually doomed multitudes of human beings and great quantities of useful goods to the destruction of wars. In our time, the relative importance of armed conflicts has even increased; it has taken on the disastrous proportions of which we are aware.

Recent history is the result of the soaring growth of industrial activity. At first this prolific movement restrained martial activity by absorbing the main part of the excess: The development of modern industry yielded the period of relative peace from 1815 to 1914.[3] Developing in this way, increasing the resources, the productive forces made possible in the same period the rapid demographic expansion of the advanced countries (this is the fleshly aspect of the bony proliferation of the factories). But in the long run the growth that the technical changes made possible became difficult to sustain. It became productive of an increased surplus itself. The First World War broke out before its limits were really reached, even locally. The Second did not itself signify that the system could not develop further (either extensively or in any case intensively). But it weighed the possibilities of a halt in development and ceased to enjoy the opportunities of a growth that nothing opposed. It is sometimes denied that the industrial plethora was at the origin of these recent wars, particularly the first. Yet it was this plethora that both wars exuded; its size was what gave them their extraordinary intensity. Consequently, the general principle of an excess of energy to be expended, considered (beyond the too narrow scope of the economy) as the effect of a movement that surpasses it, tragically illuminates a set of facts; moreover, it takes on a significance that no one can deny. We can express the hope of avoiding a war that already threatens. But in order to do so we must divert the surplus production, either into the rational extension of a difficult industrial growth, or into unproductive works that will dissipate an energy that cannot be accumulated in any case. This raises numerous problems, which are exhaustingly complex.[4] One can be skeptical of arriving easily at the practical solutions they demand, but the interest they hold is unquestionable.

I will simply state, without waiting further, that the extension of economic growth itself requires the overturning of economic principles — the overturning of the ethics that grounds them. Changing from the perspectives of *restrictive* economy to those of *general* economy actually accomplishes a Copernican transformation: a reversal of thinking — and of ethics. If a part of wealth (subject to a rough estimate) is doomed to destruction or at least to unproductive use without any possible profit, it is logical, even *inescapable*, to surrender commodities without return. Henceforth, leaving aside pure and simple dissipation, analogous to the construction of the Pyramids, the possibility of pursuing growth is itself subordinated to giving: The industrial development of the entire world demands of Americans that they lucidly grasp the necessity, for an economy such as theirs, of having a margin of profitless operations. An immense industrial network cannot be managed in the same way that one changes a tire.... It expresses a circuit of cosmic energy on which it depends, which it cannot limit, and whose laws it cannot ignore without consequences. Woe to those who, to the very end, insist on regulating the movement that exceeds them with the narrow mind of the mechanic who changes a tire.

Laws of General Economy

The Superabundance of Biochemical Energy and Growth

That as a rule an organism has at its disposal greater energy resources than are necessary for the operations that sustain life (functional activities and, in animals, essential muscular exercises, the search for food) is evident from functions like growth and reproduction. Neither growth nor reproduction would be possible if plants and animals did not normally dispose of an excess. The very principle of living matter requires that the chemical operations of life, which demand an expenditure of energy, be gainful, productive of surpluses.

Let us consider a domestic animal, a calf. (In order not to go too deeply into the matter, I will first leave aside the different contributions of animal or human energy that enable its food to be produced; every organism depends on the contribution of others, and if this contribution is favorable, it extracts the necessary energy from it, but without it the organism would soon die.) Functional activity utilizes part of the available energy, but the animal commands an excess that ensures its growth. Under normal conditions, a part of this excess is lost in comings and goings, but if the stock grower manages to keep it inactive, the

27

volume of the calf benefits; the saving appears in the form of fat. If the calf is not killed the moment comes when the reduced growth no longer consumes all of an increased excess; the calf then reaches sexual maturity; its vital forces are devoted mainly to the turbulence of the bull in the case of a male, or to pregnancy and the production of milk in the case of a female. In a sense, reproduction signifies a passage from individual growth to that of a group. If the male is castrated, its individual volume again increases for a time and a considerable amount of work is extracted from it.

In nature there is no artificial fattening of the newborn, nor is there castration. It was convenient for me to choose a domestic animal as an example, but the movements of animal matter are basically the same in all cases. On the whole, the excess energy provides for the growth or the turbulence of individuals. The calf and the cow, the bull and the ox merely add a richer and more familiar illustration of this great movement.

Plants manifest the same excess, but it is much more pronounced in their case. They are nothing but growth and reproduction (the energy necessary for their functional activity is neglible). But this indefinite exuberance must be considered in relation to the conditions that make it possible — and that limit it.

The Limits of Growth

I will speak briefly about the most general conditions of life, dwelling on one crucially important fact: Solar energy is the source of life's exuberant development. The origin and essence of our wealth are given in the radiation of the sun, which dispenses energy — wealth — without any return. The sun gives without ever receiving. Men were conscious of this long before astrophysics measured that ceaseless prodigality; they saw it ripen the harvests and they associated its splendor with the act of someone who gives without receiving. It is necessary at this point to note a dual origin of moral judgments. In former times value was given to unproductive glory, whereas in our day it is measured in terms of production: Precedence is given to energy acquisition over energy expenditure. Glory itself is justified by the consequences of a glorious deed in the sphere of utility. But, dominated though it is by practical judgment and Christian morality, the archaic sensibility is still alive: In particular it reappears in the romantic protest against the bourgeois world; only in the classical conceptions of the economy does it lose its rights entirely.

Solar radiation results in a superabundance of energy on the surface of the globe. But, first, living matter receives this energy and accumulates it within the limits given by the space that is available to it. It then radiates or squanders it, but before devoting an appreciable share to this radiation it makes maximum use of it for growth. Only the impossibility of continuing growth makes way for squander. Hence the real excess does not begin until the growth of the individual or group has reached its limits.

The immediate limitation, for each individual or each group, is given by the other individuals or other groups. But the terrestrial sphere (to be exact, the *biosphere*[5]), which corresponds to the space available to life, is the only real limit. The *individual* or group can be reduced by another individual or another group, but the total volume of living nature is not changed; in short, it is the size of the terrestrial space that limits overall growth.

Pressure

As a rule the surface of the globe is invested by life to the extent possible. By and large the myriad forms of life adapt it to the available resources, so that space is its basic limit. Certain disadvantaged areas, where the chemical operations essential to life cannot take place, seem to have no real existence. But taking into account

29

a constant relation of the biomass to the local climatic and geo-logical conditions, life occupies all the available space. These local conditions determine the intensity of the *pressure* exerted in all directions by life. But one can speak of pressure in this sense only if, by some means, the available space is increased; this space will be immediately occupied in the same way as the adjoining space. Moreover, the same is true every time life is destroyed at some point on the globe, by a forest fire, by a volcanic phenomenon or by the hand of man. The most familiar example is that of a path that a gardener clears and maintains. Once abandoned, the pressure of the surrounding life soon covers it over again with weeds and bushes swarming with animal life.

If the path is paved with asphalt, it is for a long time sheltered from the pressure. This means that the volume of life possible, assuming that the path were abandoned instead of being covered with asphalt, will not be realized, that the additional energy cor-responding to this volume is lost, is dissipated in some way. This pressure cannot be compared to that of a closed boiler. If the space is completely occupied, if there is no outlet anywhere, nothing bursts; but the pressure is there. In a sense, life suffocates within limits that are too close; it aspires in manifold ways to an impos-sible growth; it releases a steady flow of excess resources, possi-bly involving large squanderings of energy. The limit of growth being reached, life, without being in a closed container, at least enters into ebullition: Without exploding, its extreme exuber-ance pours out in a movement always bordering on explosion.

The consequences of this situation do not easily enter into our calculations. We calculate our interests, but this situation baffles us: The very word *interest* is contradictory with the *desire* at stake under these conditions. As soon as we want to act reasonably we have to consider the *utility* of our actions; utility implies an advan-tage, a maintenance or growth. Now, if it is necessary to respond to exuberance, it is no doubt possible to *use* it for growth. But the problem raised precludes this. Supposing there is no longer any growth possible, what is to be done with the seething energy that remains? To waste it is obviously not to use it. And yet, what we have is a draining-away, a pure and simple loss, *which occurs in any case*: From the first, the excess energy, if it cannot be used for growth, is lost. Moreover, in no way can this inevitable loss be accounted useful. It is only a matter of an acceptable loss, preferable to another that is regarded as unacceptable: a question of *acceptability*, not utility. Its consequences are decisive, however.

The First Effect of Pressure: Extension

It is hard to define and precisely represent the pressure thus exerted. It is both complex and elusive, but one can describe its effects. An image comes to mind, then, but I must say in offering it that it illustrates the consequences yet does not give a concrete idea of the cause.

Imagine an immense crowd assembled in the expectation of witnessing a bullfight that will take place in a bullring that is too small. The crowd wants badly to enter but cannot be entirely accommodated: Many people must wait outside. Similarly, the possibilities of life cannot be realized indefinitely; they are limited by the space, just as the entry of the crowd is limited by the number of seats in the bullring.

A first effect of the pressure will be to increase the number of seats in the bullring.

If the security service is well-organized, this number is limited precisely. But outside there may be trees and lampposts from the top of which the arena is visible. If there is no regulation against it, there will be people who will climb these trees and lampposts. Similarly, the earth first opens to life the primary space of the waters and the surface of the ground. But life quickly takes possession of the air. To start with, it was important to enlarge the surface of the green substance of plants, which absorbs the radiant energy of light. The superposition of leaves in the air extends the volume of this substance considerably: In particular, the structure of trees develops this possibility well beyond the level of the grasses. For their part the winged insects and the birds, in the wake of the pollens, invade the air.

The Second Effect of Pressure: Squander or Luxury

But the lack of room can have another effect: A fight may break out at the entrance. If lives are lost the excess of individuals over the number of seats will decrease. This effect works in a sense contrary to the first one. Sometimes the pressure results in the clearing of a new space, other times in the erasing of possibilities in excess of the available room. This last effect operates in nature in the most varied forms.

The most remarkable is death. As we know, death is not necessary. The simple forms of life are immortal: The birth of an organism reproduced through scissiparity is lost in the mists of time. Indeed, it cannot be said to have had parents. Take for example the doubles A' and A'', resulting from the splitting in two of A; A has not ceased living with the coming into being of A'; A' is still A (and the same is true of A''). But let us suppose (this is purely theoretical, for the purpose of demonstration) that in the beginning of life there was just one of these infinitesimal creatures: It would nonetheless have quickly populated the earth with its species. After a short time, in theory, reproduction would have become impossible for lack of room, and the energy it utilizes would have dissipated, e.g., in the form of heat. Moreover, this is what happens to one of these micro-organisms, duckweed, which covers a pond with a green film, after which it remains in equilibrium. For the duckweed, space is given within the narrowly determined limits of a pond. But the stagnation of the duckweed is not conceivable on the scale of the entire globe, where in any case the necessary equilibrium is lacking. It can be granted (theoretically) that a pressure everywhere equal to itself would result in a state of rest, in a general substitution of heat loss for reproduction. But real pressure has different results: It puts unequal organisms in competition with one another, and although we cannot say how the species take part in the dance, we can say what the dance is.

Besides the external action of life (climatic or volcanic phenomena), the unevenness of pressure in living matter continually makes available to growth the place left vacant by death. It is not a new space, and if one considers life as a whole, there is not really growth but a maintenance of volume in general. In other words, the possible growth is reduced to a compensation for the destructions that are brought about.

I insist on the fact that there is generally no growth but only a luxurious squandering of energy in every form! The history of life on earth is mainly the effect of a wild exuberance; the dominant event is the development of luxury, the production of increasingly burdensome forms of life.

The Three Luxuries of Nature:
Eating, Death and Sexual Reproduction
The eating of one species by another is the simplest form of luxury. The populations that were trapped by the German army acquired, thanks to the food shortage, a vulgarized knowledge of this burdensome character of the indirect development of living matter. If one cultivates potatoes or wheat, the land's yield in consumable calories is much greater than that of livestock in milk and meat for an equivalent acreage of pasture. The least burdensome form of life is that of a green micro-organism (absorbing the

33

sun's energy through the action of chlorophyll), but generally vegetation is less burdensome than animal life. Vegetation quickly
occupies the available space. Animals make it a field of slaughter
and extend its possibilities in this way; they themselves develop
more slowly. In this respect, the wild beast is at the summit: Its
continual depredations of depredators represent an immense
squandering of energy. William Blake asked the tiger: "In what
distant deeps or skies burned the fire of thine eyes?" What struck
him in this way was the cruel pressure, at the limits of possibility,
the tiger's immense power of consumption of life. In the general
effervescence of life, the tiger is a point of extreme incandescence.
And this incandescence did in fact burn first in the remote depths
of the sky, in the sun's consumption.

Eating brings death, but in an accidental form. *Of all conceivable luxuries, death, in its fatal and inexorable form, is undoubtedly
the most costly*. The fragility, the complexity, of the animal body
already exhibits its luxurious quality, but this fragility and luxury culminate in death. Just as in space the trunks and branches
of the tree raise the superimposed stages of the foliage to the
light, death distributes the passage of the generations over time.
It constantly leaves the necessary room for the coming of the
newborn, and we are wrong to curse *the one without whom we
would not exist*.

In reality, when we curse death we only fear ourselves: The
severity of *our will* is what makes us tremble. We lie to ourselves
when we dream of escaping the movement of luxurious exuberance of which we are only the most intense form. Or perhaps we
only lie to ourselves in the beginning the better to experience
the severity of this will afterward, carrying it to the rigorous
extreme of consciousness.

In this respect, the luxury of death is regarded by us in the
same way as that of sexuality, first as a negation of ourselves,

then — in a sudden reversal — as the profound truth of that movement of which life is the manifestation.

Under the present conditions, independently of our consciousness, sexual reproduction is, together with eating and death, one of the great luxurious detours that ensure the intense consumption of energy. To begin with, it accentuates that which scissiparity announced: the division by which the individual being foregoes growth for himself and, through the multiplication of individuals, transfers it to the impersonality of life. This is because, from the first, sexuality differs from miserly growth: If, with regard to the species, sexuality appears as a growth, in principle it is nevertheless the luxury of individuals. This characteristic is more accentuated in sexual reproduction, where the individuals engendered are clearly separate from those that engender them and *give* them life as one *gives to others*. But without renouncing a subsequent return to the principle of growth for the period of nutrition, the reproduction of the higher animals has not ceased to deepen the fault that separates it from the simple tendency to eat in order to increase volume and power. For these animals sexual reproduction is the occasion of a sudden and frantic squandering of energy resources, carried in a moment to the limit of possibility (in time what the tiger is in space). This squandering goes far beyond what would be sufficient for the growth of the species. It appears to be the most that an individual has the strength to accomplish in a given moment. It leads to the wholesale destruction of property — in spirit, the destruction of bodies as well — and ultimately connects up with the senseless luxury and excess of death.

Extension Through Labor and Technology, and the Luxury of Man

Man's activity is basically conditioned by this general movement

35

of life. In a sense, *in extension*, his activity opens up a new possibility to life, a new space (as did tree branches and bird wings in nature). The space that labor and technical know-how open to the increased reproduction of men is not, in the proper sense, one that life has not yet populated. But human activity transforming the world augments the mass of living matter with supplementary apparatuses, composed of an immense quantity of inert matter, which considerably increases the resources of available energy. From the first, man has the option of utilizing part of the available energy for the growth (not biological but technical) of his energy wealth. The techniques have in short made it possible to extend — to develop — the elementary movement of growth that life realizes within the limits of the possible. Of course, this development is neither continuous nor boundless. Sometimes the cessation of development corresponds to a stagnation of techniques; other times, the invention of new techniques leads to a resurgence. The growth of energy resources can itself serve as the basis of a resumption of biological (demographic) growth. The history of Europe in the nineteenth century is the best (and best known) illustration of these vast living proliferations of which technical equipment is the ossature: We are aware of the extent of the population growth linked at first to the rise of industry.

In actual fact the quantitative relations of population and toolmaking — and, in general, the conditions of economic development in history — are subject to so many interferences that it is always difficult to determine their exact distribution. In any case, I cannot incorporate detailed analyses into an overall survey that seems the only way of outlining the vast movement which animates the earth. But the recent decline in demographic growth by itself reveals the complexity of the effects. The fact is that the revivals of development that are due to human activity, that are made possible or maintained by new techniques, always have a double effect: Initially, they use a portion of the surplus energy, but then they produce a larger and larger surplus. This surplus eventually contributes to making growth more difficult, for growth no longer suffices to use it up. At a certain point the advantage of extension is neutralized by the contrary advantage, that of luxury; the former remains operative, but in a disappointing – uncertain, often powerless – way. The drop in the demographic curves is perhaps the first indicator of the change of sign that has occurred: Henceforth what matters *primarily* is no longer to develop the productive forces but to spend their products sumptuously.

At this point, immense squanderings are about to take place: After a century of populating and of industrial peace, the temporary limit of development being encountered, the two world wars organized the greatest orgies of wealth – and of human beings – that history has recorded. Yet these orgies coincide with an appreciable rise in the general standard of living: The majority of the population benefits from more and more unproductive services; work is reduced and wages are increased overall.

Thus, man is only a roundabout, subsidiary response to the problem of growth. Doubtless, through labor and technique, he has made possible an extension of growth beyond the given limits. But just as the herbivore relative to the plant, and the carnivore relative to the herbivore, is a luxury, man is the most suited of all living beings to consume intensely, sumptuously, the excess energy offered up by the pressure of life to conflagrations befitting the solar origins of its movement.

The Accursed Share
This truth is paradoxical, to the extent of being exactly contrary to the usual perception.

This paradoxical character is underscored by the fact that, even at the highest point of exuberance, its significance is still veiled.

37

Under present conditions, everything conspires to obscure the basic movement that tends to restore wealth to its function, to gift-giving, to squandering without reciprocation. On the one hand, mechanized warfare, producing its ravages, characterizes this movement as something alien, hostile to human will. On the other hand, the raising of the standard of living is in no way represented as a requirement of luxury. The movement that demands it is even a protest against the luxury of the great fortunes: thus the demand made in the name of *justice*. Without having anything against justice, obviously, one may be allowed to point out that here the word conceals the profound truth of its contrary, which is precisely *freedom*. Under the mask of justice, it is true that general *freedom* takes on the lackluster and neutral appearance of existence subjected to the necessities: If anything, it is a narrowing of limits *to what is most just*; it is not a dangerous breaking-loose, a meaning that the word has lost. It is a guarantee against the risk of servitude, not a will to assume those risks without which there is no freedom.

Opposition of the "General" Viewpoint to the "Particular" Viewpoint

Of course, the fact of being afraid, of turning away from a movement of dilapidation, which impels us and even *defines* us, is not surprising. The consequences of this movement are distressing from the start. The image of the tiger reveals the truth of eating. Death has become our horror, and though in a sense the fact of being carnivorous and of facing death bravely answers to the demand of virility (but that is a different matter!); sexuality is linked to the scandals of death and the eating of meat.[6]

But this atmosphere of malediction presupposes anguish, and anguish for its part signifies the absence (or weakness) of the pressure exerted by the exuberance of life. Anguish arises when the anxious individual is not himself stretched tight by the feeling of superabundance. This is precisely what evinces the isolated, individual character of anguish. There can be anguish only from a personal, *particular* point of view that is radically opposed to the *general* point of view based on the exuberance of living matter as a whole. Anguish is meaningless for someone who overflows with life, and for life as a whole, which is an overflowing by its very nature.

As for the present historical situation, it is characterized by the fact that judgments concerning the *general* situation proceed from a *particular* point of view. As a rule, *particular* existence always risks succumbing for lack of resources. It contrasts with *general* existence whose resources are in excess and for which death has no meaning. From the *particular* point of view, the problems are posed *in the first instance* by a deficiency of resources. They are posed *in the first instance* by an excess of resources if one starts from the *general* point of view. Doubtless the problem of extreme poverty remains in any case. Moreover, it should be understood that *general economy* must also, whenever possible and first of all, envisage the development of growth. But if it considers poverty or growth, it takes into account the limits that the one and the other cannot fail to encounter and the dominant (decisive) character of the problems that follow from the existence of surpluses.

Briefly considering an example, the problem of extreme poverty in India cannot immediately be dissociated from the demographic growth of that country, or from the lack of proportion with its industrial development. India's possibilities of industrial growth cannot themselves be dissociated from the excesses of American resources. A typical problem of *general economy* emerges from this situation. On the one hand, there appears the need for an exudation; on the other hand, the need for a growth. The present state of the world is defined by the unevenness of the (quantitative or qualitative) pressure exerted by human life. General

39

economy suggests, therefore, as a correct operation, a transfer of American wealth to India without reciprocation. This proposal takes into account the threat to America that would result from the pressure — and the imbalances of pressure — exerted in the world by the developments of Hindu life.

These considerations necessarily give first priority to the problem of war, which can be clearly regarded only in the light of a fundamental ebullition. The only solution is in raising the global standard of living under the current moral conditions, the only means of absorbing the American surplus, thereby reducing the pressure to below the danger point.

This theoretical conception differs little from the empirical views that have recently appeared concerning the subject, but it is more radical, and it is interesting to note that these views have agreed with the above ideas, which were conceived earlier: This confirmation gives added strength, it seems, to both contradictions.

The Solutions of General Economy and "Self-Consciousness"

But it has to be added at once that, however well-defined the solutions, their implementation on the required scale is so difficult that from the outset the undertaking hardly looks encouraging. The theoretical solution exists; indeed, its necessity is far from escaping the notice of those on whom the decision seems to depend. Nevertheless, and even more clearly, what *general economy* defines first is the explosive character of this world, carried to the extreme degree of explosive tension in the present time. A curse obviously weighs on human life insofar as it does not have the strength to control a vertiginous movement. It must be stated as a principle, without hesitation, that the lifting of such a curse depends on man and *only on man*. But it cannot be lifted if the movement from which it emanates does not appear clearly *in con-*

sciousness. In this regard it seems rather disappointing to have nothing more to propose, as a remedy for the catastrophe that threatens, than the "raising of the living standard." This recourse, as I have said, is linked to a *refusal to see*, in its *truth*, the exigency to which the recourse is intended to respond.

Yet if one considers at the same time the weakness and the virtue of this solution, two things become immediately apparent: that it is the only one capable of rather wide acceptance; and that, due to its equivocal nature, it provokes and stimulates an effort of lucidity all the greater for seeming to be far removed from such an effort. In this way the avoidance of the truth ensures, in reciprocal fashion, a recognition of the truth. In any case, the mind of contemporary man would be reluctant to embrace solutions that, not being negative, were emphatic and arbitrary; it prefers that exemplary rigor of consciousness which alone may slowly make human life commensurate with its truth. The exposition of a *general economy* implies intervention in public affairs, certainly; but first of all and more profoundly, what it aims at is consciousness, what it looks to from the outset is the *self-consciousness* that man would finally achieve in the lucid vision of its linked historical forms.

Thus, *general economy* begins with an account of the historical data, relating their meaning to the *present data*.

PART TWO

The Historical Data I

The Society of Consumption

Sacrifices and Wars of the Aztecs

Society of Consumption and Society of Enterprise

I will describe sets of social facts manifesting a general movement of the economy.

I want to state a principle from the outset: By definition, this movement, the effect of which is prodigality, is far from being equal to itself. While there is an excess of resources over needs (meaning real needs, such that a society would suffer if they were not satisfied), this excess is not always consumed to no purpose. Society can grow, in which case the excess is deliberately reserved for growth. Growth regularizes; it channels a disorderly effervescence into the regularity of productive operations. But growth, to which is tied the development of knowledge, is by nature a transitory state. It cannot continue indefinitely. Man's science obviously has to correct the perspectives that result from the historical conditions of its elaboration. Nothing is more different from man enslaved to the operations of growth than the relatively free man of stable societies. The character of human life changes the moment it ceases to be guided by fantasy and begins to meet the demands of undertakings that ensure the proliferation of given works. In the same way, the face of a man changes if he goes from the turbulence of the night to the serious business of the morning. The serious humanity of growth becomes civilized, more gentle, but it tends to confuse gentleness with the value of life, and life's tranquil duration with its poetic dynamism. Under these conditions the clear knowledge it generally has of things cannot become a full self-knowledge. It is misled by what it takes for full humanity, that is, humanity at work, living in order to work without ever fully enjoying the fruits of its labor. Of course, the man who is relatively idle or at least unconcerned about his achievements — the type discussed in both ethnography and history — is not a consummate man either. But he helps us to gauge that which we lack.

Consumption in the Aztec Worldview

The Aztecs, about whom I will speak first, are poles apart from us morally. As a civilization is judged by its works, their civilization seems wretched to us. They used writing and were versed in astronomy, but all their important undertakings were useless: Their science of architecture enabled them to construct pyramids on top of which they immolated human beings.

Their world view is singularly and diametrically opposed to the activity-oriented perspective that we have. Consumption loomed just as large in their thinking as production does in ours. They were just as concerned about *sacrificing* as we are about *working*.

The sun himself was in their eyes the expression of sacrifice. He was a god resembling man. He had become the sun by hurling himself into the flames of a brazier.

The Spanish Franciscan Bernardino de Sahagún, who wrote in the middle of the sixteenth century, reports what some old Aztecs told him:

It is said that before the light of day existed, the gods assem-

46

bled at the place called Teotihaucan...and spoke among themselves, saying: "Who will take it upon himself to bring light to the world?" On hearing these words, a god called Tecuciztecatl presented himself and replied: "I will be the one. I will bring light to the world." The gods then spoke again and said: "Who else among you?" They looked at one another then, wondering who this would be, and none dared accept the charge; all were afraid and made excuses. One of the gods who usually went unnoticed did not say anything but only listened to what the other gods were saying. The others spoke to him, saying, "Let it be you, *bubosito*." And he gladly accepted, replying: "I receive your order gratefully; so be it." And the two that were chosen began immediately to do penance, which lasted four days. Then a fire was lit in a hearth made in a rock.... The god named Tecuciztecatl only offered costly things. Instead of branches he offered rich feathers called *quetzalli*; instead of grass balls he offered gold ones; instead of maguey spines he offered spines made with precious stones; and instead of bloodied spines he offered spines of red coral. And the copal he offered was of a very high quality. The *buboso*, whose name was Nanauatzin, offered nine green water rushes bound in threes, instead of ordinary branches. He offered balls of grass and maguey spines bloodied with his own blood, and instead of copal he offered the scabs of his *bubas*.

A tower was made for each of these two gods, in the form of a hill. On these hills they did penance for four nights.... After the four nights of penance were completed, the branches and all the other objects they had used were thrown down there. The following night, a little before midnight, when they were to do their office, Tecuciztecatl was given his adornments. These consisted of a headdress of *aztacomitl* feathers and a sleeveless jacket. As for Nanauatzin, the *buboso*, they tied a paper headdress, called *amatzontli*, on his hair and gave him a paper stole and a paper rag for pants to wear. When midnight had come, all the gods gathered round the hearth, which was called *teotexcalli*, where the fire had burned for four days.

They separated into two lines on the two sides of the fire. The two chosen ones took their places near the hearth, with their faces to the fire, in the middle of the two lines of gods. The latter were all standing and they spoke to Tecuciztecatl, saying: "Go on, Tecuciztecatl. Cast yourself into the fire!" Hearing this, he started to throw himself into the flames, but the fire was burning high and very hot, and he stopped in fear and drew back. A second time he gathered his strength and turned to throw himself into the fire, but when he got near he stopped and did not dare go further; four times he tried, but could not. Now, it had been ordered that no one could try more than four times, so when the four attempts had been made the gods addressed Nanauatzin, saying: "Go on, Nanauatzin. It is your turn to try!" As soon as these words were said, he shut his eyes and, taking courage, went forward and threw himself into the fire. He began at once to crackle and sizzle like something being roasted. Seeing that he had thrown himself into the fire and was burning, Tecuciztecatl also cast himself into the flames and burned. It is said that an eagle went into the fire at the same time and burned, and this is why the eagle has scorched-looking and blackened feathers. An ocelot followed thereafter but did not burn, only being singed, and this is why the ocelot remains spotted black and white.[1]

A short while later, having fallen on their knees, the gods saw Nanauatzin, "who had become the sun," rising in the East. "He looked very red, appearing to sway from side to side, and none of them could keep their eyes on him, because he blinded them with his light. He shone brightly with his rays that reached in all directions." The moon in turn rose up over the horizon. Because he had hesitated, Tecuciztecatl shone less brightly. Then the gods had to die; the wind, Quetzalcoatl, killed them all: The wind tore out their hearts and used them to animate the newborn stars.

This myth is paralleled by the belief that not only men but also wars were created "so that there would be people whose hearts and blood could be taken so that the sun might eat."[2] Like the myth, this belief obviously conveys an extreme value placed on consumption. Each year, in honor of the sun, the Mexicans observed the four days of fasting that were observed by the gods. Then they immolated lepers who were like the *buboso* with his skin disease. For in their minds thought was only an exposition of actions.

The Human Sacrifices of Mexico

We have a fuller, more vivid knowledge of the human sacrifices of Mexico than we do of those of earlier times; doubtless they represent an apex of horror in the cruel chain of religious rites.

The priests killed their victims on top of the pyramids. They would stretch them over a stone altar and strike them in the chest with an obsidian knife. They would tear out the still-beating heart and raise it thus to the sun. Most of the victims were prisoners of war, which justified the idea of wars as necessary to the life of the sun: Wars meant consumption, not conquest, and the Mexicans thought that if they ceased the sun would cease to give light.

"Around Easter time," they undertook the sacrificial slaying of a young man of irreproachable beauty. He was chosen from among the captives the previous year, and from that moment he lived like a great lord. "He went through the whole town very

49

well dressed, with flowers in his hand and accompanied by certain personalities. He would bow graciously to all whom he met, and they all knew he was the image of Tezcatlipoca [one of the greatest gods] and prostrated themselves before him, worshipping him wherever they met him."[3] Sometimes he could be seen in the temple on top of the pyramid of Quauhxicalco: "Up there he would play the flute at night or in the daytime, whichever time he wished to do it. After playing the flute, he too would turn incense toward the four parts of the world, and then return home, to his room."[4] Every care was taken to ensure the elegance and princely distinction of his life. "If, due to the good treatment he grew stout, they would make him drink salt-water to keep slender."[5] "Twenty days previous to the festival they gave this youth four maidens, well prepared and educated for this purpose. During those twenty days he had carnal intercourse with these maidens. The four girls they gave him as wives and who had been reared with special care for that purpose were given names of four goddesses.... Five days before he was to die they gave festivities for him, banquets held in cool and gay places, and many chieftains and prominent people accompanied him. On the day of the festival when he was to die they took him to an oratory, which they called Tlacuchcalco. Before reaching it, at a place called Tlapituoaian, the women stepped aside and left him. As he got to the place where he was to be killed, he mounted the steps by himself and on each one of these he broke one of the flutes which he had played during the year."[6] "He was awaited at the top by the satraps or priests who were to kill him, and these now grabbed him and threw him onto the stone block, and, holding him by feet, hands and head, thrown on his back, the priest who had the stone knife buried it with a mighty thrust in the victim's breast and, after drawing it out, thrust one hand into the opening and tore out the heart, which he at once offered to the sun."[7]

Respect was shown for the young man's body: It was carried down slowly to the temple courtyard. Ordinary victims were thrown down the steps to the bottom. The greatest violence was habitual. The dead person was flayed and the priest then clothed himself in this bloody skin. Men were thrown into a furnace and pulled out with a hook to be placed on the executioner's block still alive. More often that not the flesh consecrated by the immolation was eaten. The festivals followed one another without interruption and every year the divine service called for countless sacrifices: Twenty thousand is given as the number. One of the victims incarnating a god, he climbed to the sacrifice surrounded, like a god, by an attendance that would accompany him in death.

Intimacy of Executioners and Victims

The Aztecs observed a singular conduct with those who were about to die. They treated these prisoners humanely, giving them the food and drink they asked for. Concerning a warrior who brought back a captive, then offered him in sacrifice, it was said that he had "considered his captive as his own flesh and blood, calling him son, while the latter called him father."[8] The victims would dance and sing with those who brought them to die. Efforts were often made to relieve their anguish. A woman incarnating the "mother of the gods" was consoled by the healers and midwives who said to her: "Don't be sad, fair friend; you will spend this night with the king, so you can rejoice." It was not made clear to her that she was to be killed, because death needed to be sudden and unexpected in her case. Ordinarily the condemned prisoners were well aware of their fate and were forced to stay up the final night, singing and dancing. Sometimes they were made to drink until drunk or, to drive away the idea of impending death, they were given a concubine.

This difficult wait for death was borne better by some victims than by others. Concerning the slaves who were to die during one of the November festivals, we are told that "they went to the homes of their masters to bid them good-bye.... They were singing in a very loud voice, so loud that it seemed to split their breast, and upon reaching the house of their masters they dipped both hands in the bowls of paint or of ink and put them on the lintels of the doors and the posts of the houses, leaving their imprint in colors; the same they did in the houses of their relatives. Some of them who were lion-hearted would eat as usual, others could not eat thinking of the death they soon would have to suffer."[9] A slave who represented the goddess Illamatecutli was dressed entirely in white, adorned with white and black feathers, and her face was painted half black and half white. "Previous to being killed, this woman had to dance, and the old men played the tune for this dance, and the singers sang the songs; and while she danced she cried, sighed and worried, knowing that her death was so close at hand."[10] In the autumn women were sacrificed in a temple called Coatlan. "Some of them, upon climbing the steps, were singing, others screamed, and still others cried."[11]

The Religious Character of the Wars

These sacrifices of prisoners cannot be understood apart from the conditions that made them possible: wars and the assumed risk of death. The Mexicans shed blood only provided that they risked dying.

They were conscious of this enchantment of war and sacrifice. The midwife would cut the umbilical cord of the newborn baby boy and say to him:

> I cut your navel in the middle of your body. Know and understand that the house in which you are born is not your dwelling.... It is your cradle, the place where you lay your head....

52

Your true land is elsewhere; you are promised for other places. You belong to the countryside where battles are fought; you were sent to go there; your function and your skill is warfare; your duty is to give the sun the blood of your enemies to drink and to supply the earth with the bodies of your enemies to eat. As for your native land, your legacy and your happiness, you will find them in the house of the sun in the sky.... You will be fortunate to be found worthy of dying on the battle-field, decorated with flowers. What I now cut from your body and from the middle of your stomach rightly belongs to Tlatecutli who is the earth and the sun. When war begins to seethe and the soldiers assemble, we shall put it in the hands of those who are valorous soldiers, so that they might give it to your father and mother, the earth and the sun. They will bury it in the middle of the field where the battles are fought: This will be the proof that you are offered and promised to the earth and the sun; this will be the sign that you profess this office of warfare, and your name will be written in the field of battle so that your name and your person will not be forgotten. This precious offering collected from your body is like the offering of a maguey spine, of reeds for smoking and *axcoyatl* branches. Through it your vow and sacrifice are confirmed....[12]

The individual who brought back a captive had just as much of a share in the sacred office as the priest. A first bowl of the victim's blood, drained from the wound, was offered to the sun by the priests. A second bowl was collected by the sacrificer. The latter would go before the images of the gods and wet their lips with the warm blood. The body of the sacrificed was his by right; he would carry it home, setting aside the head, and the rest would be eaten at a banquet, cooked without salt or spices — but eaten by the invited guests, not by the sacrificer, who regarded his victim as a son, as a second self. At the dance that ended the feast, the warrior would hold the victim's head in his hand.

If the warrior had himself been overcome instead of returning a victor, his death on the field of battle would have had the same meaning as the ritual sacrifice of his prisoner: It would also have satisfied the hungry gods.

This was said in the prayer to Tezcatlipoca for the soldiers: "In truth, you are not wrong to want them to die in battle, for you did not send them into this world for any other purpose than to serve as food for the sun and the earth, with their blood and their flesh."[13]

Satiated with blood and flesh, the sun gave glory to the soul in his palace. There the war dead mingled with the immolated prisoners. The meaning of death in combat was brought out in the same prayer: "Make them bold and courageous; remove all weakness from their hearts so that they may not only receive death joyfully, but desire it and find charm and sweetness therein; so that they do not fear arrows or swords but rather consider them a pleasant thing, as if they were flowers and exquisite dishes of food."

From the Primacy of Religion to the Primacy of Military Effectiveness

The value of warfare in Mexican society cannot mislead us: It was not a *military* society. Religion remained the obvious key to its workings. If the Aztecs must be situated, they belong among the warrior societies, in which pure, uncalculated violence and the ostentatious forms of combat held sway. The reasoned organization of war and conquest was unknown to them. A truly *military* society is a venture society, for which war means a development of power, an orderly progression of empire.[14] It is a relatively mild society; it makes a custom of the rational principles of enterprise, whose purpose is given in the future, and it excludes the

54

madness of sacrifice. There is nothing more contrary to military organization than these squanderings of wealth represented by hecatombs of slaves.

And yet the extreme importance of warfare had brought about a significant change for the Aztecs, in the direction of the *rationality* of enterprise (which introduces, together with the concern for results and for effective force, a beginning of humanity) as against the cruel *violence* of consumption. While "the king remained in his palace," the court favored the victim (who was given "the honors of a god") with one of the most solemn sacrifices of the year. There is no possibility of a mistake here: This was a sacrifice of substitution. A softening of the ritual had occurred, shifting onto others the internal violence that is the moral principle of consumption. To be sure, the movement of violence that animated Aztec society was never turned more within than without; but internal and external violences combined in an economy that put nothing in reserve. The ritual sacrifices of prisoners commanded the sacrifices of warriors; the sacrificed victims represented at least the sumptuary expenditure of the sacrificer. The substituting of a prisoner for the king was an obvious, if inconsequent, abatement of this sacrificial frenzy.

Sacrifice or Consumption

This softening of the sacrificial process finally discloses a movement to which the rites of immolation were a response. This movement appears to us in its logical necessity alone and we cannot know if the sequence of acts conforms to it in detail; but in any case its coherence is evident.

Sacrifice restores to the sacred world that which servile use has degraded, rendered profane. Servile use has made a *thing* (an *object*) of that which, in a deep sense, is of the same nature as the *subject*, is in a relation of intimate participation with the subject.

It is not necessary that the sacrifice actually destroy the animal or plant of which man had to make a *thing* for his use. They must at least be destroyed as things, that is, *insofar as they have become things*. Destruction is the best means of negating a utilitarian relation between man and the animal or plant. But it rarely goes to the point of holocaust. It is enough that the consumption of the offerings, or the *communion*, has a meaning that is not reducible to the shared ingestion of food. The victim of the sacrifice cannot be consumed in the same way as a motor uses fuel. What the ritual has the virtue of rediscovering is the intimate participation of the sacrificer and the victim, to which a servile use had put an end. The slave bound to labor and having become the property of another is a *thing* just as a work animal is a thing. The individual who employs the labor of his prisoner severs the tie that links him to his fellow man. He is not far from the moment when he will sell him. But the owner has not simply made a *thing*, a commodity, of this property. No one can make a *thing* of the second self that the slave is without at the same time estranging himself from his own intimate being, without giving himself the limits of a *thing*.

This should not be considered narrowly: There is no perfect operation, and neither the slave nor the master is entirely reduced to the *order of things*. The slave is a thing for the owner; he accepts this situation which he prefers to dying; he effectively loses part of his intimate value for himself, for it is not enough to be this or that: One also has to be for others. Similarly, for the slave the owner has ceased to be his fellow man; he is profoundly separated from him; even if his equals continue to see him as a man, even if he is still a man for others, he is now in a world where a man can be merely a *thing*. The same poverty then extends over human life as extends over the countryside if the weather is overcast. Overcast weather, when the sun is filtered by the clouds and the play of light goes dim, appears to "reduce things to what they are." The error is obvious: What is before me is never anything less than the universe; the universe is not a *thing* and I am not at all mistaken when I see its brilliance in the sun. But if the sun is hidden I more clearly see the barn, the field, the hedgerow. I no longer see the splendor of the light that played over the barn; rather I see this barn or this hedgerow like a screen between the universe and me.

In the same way, slavery brings into the world the absence of light that is the separate positing of each *thing*, reduced to the *use* that it has. Light, or brilliance, manifests the intimacy of life, that which life deeply is, which is perceived by the subject as being true to itself and as the transparency of the universe.

But the reduction of "that which is" to the *order of things* is not limited to slavery. Slavery is abolished, but we ourselves are aware of the aspects of social life in which man is relegated to the level of *things*, and we should know that this relegation did not await slavery. From the start, the introduction of *labor* into the world replaced intimacy, the depth of desire and its free outbreaks, with rational progression, where what matters is no longer the truth of the present moment, but, rather, the subsequent results of *operations*. The first labor established the world of *things*, to which the profane world of the Ancients generally corresponds. Once the world of things was posited, man himself became one of the things of this world, at least for the time in which he labored. It is this degradation that man has always tried to escape. In his strange myths, in his cruel rites, man is *in search of a lost intimacy* from the first.

Religion is this long effort and this anguished quest: It is always a matter of detaching from the *real* order, from the poverty of *things*, and of restoring the *divine* order. The animal or plant that man *uses* (as if they only had value *for him* and none for them-

57

selves) is restored to the truth of the intimate world; he receives a sacred communication from it, which restores him in turn to interior freedom.

The meaning of this profound freedom is given in destruction, whose essence is to consume *profitlessly* whatever might remain in the progression of useful works. Sacrifice destroys that which it consecrates. It does not have to destroy as fire does; only the tie that connected the offering to the world of profitable activity is severed, but this separation has the sense of a definitive consumption; the consecrated offering cannot be restored to the *real* order. This principle opens the way to passionate release; it liberates violence while marking off the domain in which violence reigns absolutely.

The world of *intimacy* is as antithetical to the *real* world as immoderation is to moderation, madness to reason, drunkenness to lucidity. There is moderation only in the object, reason only in the identity of the object with itself, lucidity only in the distinct knowledge of objects. The world of the subject is the night: that changeable, infinitely suspect night which, in the sleep of reason, *produces monsters. I submit that madness itself gives a rarefied idea of the free "subject," unsubordinated to the "real" order and occupied only with the present.* The *subject* leaves its own domain and subordinates itself to the *objects* of the *real* order as soon as it becomes concerned for the future. For the *subject* is consumption insofar as it is not tied down to work. If I am no longer concerned about "what will be" but about "what is," what reason do I have to keep anything in reserve? I can at once, in disorder, make an instantaneous consumption of all that I possess. This useless consumption is *what suits me*, once my concern for the morrow is removed. And if I thus consume immoderately, I reveal to my fellow beings that which I am *intimately*: Consumption is the way in which *separate* beings communicate.[15] Everything shows through, everything is open and infinite between those who consume intensely. But nothing counts then; violence is released and it breaks forth without limits, as the heat increases.

What ensures the return of the *thing* to the *intimate* order is its entry into the hearth of consumption, where the violence no doubt is limited, but never without great difficulty. It is always the purpose of sacrifice to give destruction its due, to save the rest from a mortal danger of contagion. All those who have to do with sacrifice are in danger, but its limited ritual form regularly has the effect of protecting those who offer it.

Sacrifice is heat, in which the intimacy of those who make up the system of common works is rediscovered. Violence is its principle, but the works limit it in time and space; it is subordinated to the concern for uniting and preserving the commonality. The individuals break loose, but a breaking-loose that melts them and blends them indiscriminately with their fellow beings helps to connect them together in the operations of secular time. It is not yet a matter of *enterprise*, which absorbs the excess forces with a view to the unlimited development of wealth. The works in question only aim at continuance. They only predetermine the limits of the festival (whose renewal is ensured by their fecundity, which has its source in the festival itself). But the community is saved from ruination. The *victim* is given over to violence.

The Victim, Sacred and Cursed

The victim is a surplus taken from the mass of *useful* wealth. And he can only be withdrawn from it in order to be consumed profitlessly, and therefore utterly destroyed. Once chosen, he is the *accursed share*, destined for violent consumption. But the curse tears him away from the *order of things*; it gives him a recognizable figure, which now radiates intimacy, anguish, the profundity of living beings.

Nothing is more striking than the attention that is lavished on him. Being a thing, he cannot truly be withdrawn from the real order, which binds him, unless destruction rids him of his "thinghood," eliminating his usefulness once and for all. As soon as he is consecrated and during the time between the consecration and death, he enters into the closeness of the sacrificers and participates in their consumptions: He is one of their own and in the festival in which he will perish, he sings, dances and enjoys all the pleasures with them. There is no more servility in him; he can even receive arms and fight. He is lost in the immense confusion of the festival. And that is precisely his undoing.

The victim will be the only one in fact to leave the real order entirely, for he alone is carried along to the end by the movement of the festival. The sacrificer is divine only with reservations. The future is heavily reserved in him; the future is the weight that he bears as a thing. The official theologians[16] whose tradition Sahagún collected were well aware of this, for they placed the voluntary sacrifice of Nanauatzin above the others, praised warriors for being consumed by the gods, and gave divinity the meaning of consumption. We cannot know to what extent the victims of Mexico accepted their fate. It may be that in a sense certain of them "considered it an honor" to be offered to the gods. But their immolation was not voluntary. Moreover, it is clear that, from the time of Sahagún's informants, these death orgies were tolerated because they impressed foreigners. The Mexicans immolated children that were chosen from among their own. But severe penalties had to be decreed against those who walked away from their procession when they went up to the altars. Sacrifice comprises a mixture of anguish and frenzy. The frenzy is more powerful than the anguish, but only providing its effects are diverted to the exterior, onto a foreign prisoner. It suffices for the sacrificer to give up the wealth that the victim could have been for him.

This understandable lack of rigor does not, however, change the meaning of the ritual. The only valid excess was one that went beyond the bounds, and one whose consumption appeared worthy of the gods. This was the price men paid to escape their downfall and remove the weight introduced in them by the avarice and cold calculation of the real order.

The Gift of Rivalry: "Potlatch"

The General Importance of Ostentatious Gifts in Mexican Society

Human sacrifices were only an extreme moment in the cycle of prodigalities. The passion that made the blood stream from the pyramids generally led the Aztec world to make unproductive use of a substantial portion of the resources it commanded.

One of the functions of the sovereign, of the "chief of men," who had immense riches at his disposal, was to indulge in ostentatious squander. Apparently, he himself was supposed to have been, in more ancient times, the culmination of the cycle of sacrifices: His immolation — consented to by the people he embodied, if not by him — could have given the rising tide of killings the value of an unlimited consumption. His power must have saved him in the end. But he was so clearly the man of prodigality that he gave his wealth in place of his life. He was obliged to *give* and to *play*. Sahagún writes:

> The kings looked for opportunities to show their generosity and to achieve a reputation in that regard. This is why they would contribute large sums for war or for the *areitos* [dances preceding or following sacrifices]. They would pledge very pre-

cious things in the games and, when one of the commoners, man or woman, ventured to greet them and speak a few words that pleased them, they would give food and drink, along with fabrics for wearing and sleeping. If someone else composed songs that were agreeable to them, they would give gifts that were in keeping with his merit and with the pleasure he had caused them.[17]

The sovereign was merely the richest, but everyone according to his worth and his image — the rich, the nobles, the "merchants" — had to answer to the same expectation. The festivals were an outpouring not only of blood but also of wealth in general. Each one contributed in proportion to his power and each one was offered the occasion to display his power. Through capture (in warfare) or through purchase, the warriors and the merchants obtained the victims of the sacrifices. The Mexicans built stone temples embellished with divine statues, and the ritual service multiplied the expensive offerings. The officiants and the victims were richly adorned; the ritual feasts entailed considerable expenditures.

Public festivals were given personally by the wealthy, the "merchants" in particular.[18]

The Wealthy and Ritual Prodigality

The Spanish chroniclers left precise information concerning the "merchants" of Mexico and the customs they followed, customs that must have astonished the Spaniards. These "merchants" led expeditions to unsafe territories. They often had to fight and they often prepared the way for a war, which explains the honor that attached to their profession. But the risk they assumed could not have been enough to make them the equals of the nobles. In the eyes of the Spaniards, business was demeaning, even if it led to adventure. The judgment of the Europeans derived from the principle of commerce based solely on interest. But the great "merchants" of Mexico did not exactly follow the rule of profit; their trading was conducted without bargaining and it maintained the glorious character of the trader. The Aztec "merchant" did not sell; he practiced the *gift-exchange*: He received riches as a *gift* from the "chief of men" (from the sovereign, whom the Spanish called the *king*); *he made a present* of these riches to the lords of the lands he visited. "In receiving these gifts, the great lords of that province hastened to give other presents in return ... so that they might be offered to the king...." The sovereign gave cloaks, petticoats and precious blouses. The "merchant" received as a gift for himself richly colored feathers of various shapes, cut stones of all sorts, shells, fans, shell paddles for stirring cocoa, wild-animal skins worked and ornamented with designs.[19] As for the objects the "merchants" brought back from their travels, they did not consider them to be mere commodities. On their return, they did not have them carried into their house in the daylight. "They waited for nightfall and for a favorable time. One of the days called *ce calli* (a house) was regarded as propitious because they held that the objects of which they were the bearers, entering the house on that day, would enter as sacred things and, as such, would persevere there."[20]

An article of exchange, in these practices, was not a *thing*; it was not reduced to the inertia, the lifelessness of the profane world. The *gift* that one made of it was a sign of glory, and the object itself had the radiance of glory. By giving, one exhibited one's wealth and one's good fortune (one's power). The "merchant" was the man-who-gives, so much so that his first concern on returning from an expedition was with offering a banquet to which he invited his confreres, who went home laden with presents.

This was merely a feast celebrating a return. But if "some merchant became rich and accounted himself rich, he would give a festival or a banquet for all the high-class merchants and for the lords, because it would have been considered base to die without having made some splendid expenditure that might add luster to his person by displaying the favor of the gods who had given him everything. . . ."[21] The festival began with the ingestion of an intoxicant giving visions which the guests would describe to each other once the narcosis had dissipated. For two days the master of the house would distribute food, drinks, reeds for smoking and flowers.

More rarely, a "merchant" would give a banquet during a festival called *panquetzaliztli*. This was a type of sacred and ruinous ceremony. The "merchant" who celebrated it sacrificed slaves for the occasion. He had to invite people from all around and assemble presents worth a fortune, including cloaks "numbering eight hundred thousand," waistbands "of which there were gathered four hundred of the richest and a great many others of ordinary quality."[22] The most substantial gifts went to the captains and dignitaries; the men of lesser rank received less. The people danced countless *areitos*, into which entered splendidly dressed slaves, wearing necklaces, flower garlands and rondaches decorated with flowers. They danced, taking turns smoking and smelling their fragrant reeds. Then they were placed on a platform, "so that the guests might see them better, and they were handed plates of food and drinks and attended to very graciously." When the time came for the sacrifice, the "merchant" who gave the festival dressed up like one of the slaves in order to go with them to the temple where the priests were waiting. These victims, armed for combat, had to defend themselves against the warriors who attacked them as they passed by. If one of the aggressors captured a slave, the "merchant" had to pay him the price of the slave. The sovereign himself attended the solemn sacrifice, which was followed by the shared consumption of the flesh in the house of the "merchant."[23]

These customs, the *gift exchange* in particular, are far removed from present commercial practices. Their significance becomes apparent only when we compare them with an institution still in existence, the *potlatch* of the Indians of northwestern America.

The "Potlatch" of the Indians of the American Northwest

Classical economy imagined the first exchanges in the form of barter. Why would it have thought that in the beginning a mode of acquisition such as exchange had not answered the need to acquire, but rather the contrary need to lose or squander? The classical conception is now questionable in a sense.

The "merchants" of Mexico practiced the paradoxical system of exchanges that I have described as a regular sequence of gifts; these customs, not barter, in fact constituted the archaic organization of exchange. Potlatch, still practiced by the Indians of the Northwest Coast of America, is its typical form. Ethnographers now employ this term to designate institutions functioning on a similar principle; they find traces of it in all societies. Among the Tlingit, the Haida, the Tsimshian, the Kwakiutl, potlatch is of prime importance in social life. The least advanced of these small tribes give potlatches in ceremonies marking a person's change of condition, at the time of initiations, marriages, funerals. In the more civilized tribes a potlatch is still given in the course of a festival. One can choose a festival in which to give it, but it can itself be the occasion of a festival.

Potlatch is, like commerce, a means of circulating wealth, but it excludes bargaining. More often than not it is the solemn giving of considerable riches, offered by a chief to his rival for the purpose of humiliating, challenging and obligating him. The recipient has to erase the humiliation and take up the challenge; he must satisfy the *obligation* that was contracted by accepting. He can only reply, a short time later, by means of a new potlatch, more generous than the first: He must pay back with interest.

Gift-giving is not the only form of potlatch: A rival is challenged by a solemn destruction of riches. In principle, the destruction is offered to the mythical ancestors of the donee; it is little different from a sacrifice. As recently as the nineteenth century a Tlingit chieftain would sometimes go before a rival and cut the throats of slaves in his presence. At the proper time, the destruction was repaid by the killing of a large number of slaves. The Chukchee of the Siberian Northeast have related institutions. They slaughter highly valuable dog teams, for it is necessary for them to startle, to stifle the rival group. The Indians of the Northwest Coast would set fire to their villages or break their canoes to pieces. They have emblazoned copper bars possessing a fictive value (depending on how famous or how old the coppers are): Sometimes these bars are worth a fortune. They throw them into the sea or shatter them.[24]

Theory of "Potlatch"

1. *The paradox of the "gift" reduced to the "acquisition" of a "power."*
Since the publication of Marcel Mauss's *The Gift*, the institution of potlatch has been the object of a sometimes dubious interest and curiosity. Potlatch enables one to perceive a connection between religious behaviors and economic ones. Nevertheless, one would not be able to find laws in common between these two types of behavior — if by economy one understood a conventional set of human activities, and not the general economy in its irreducible movement. It would be futile, as a matter of fact, to consider the economic aspects of potlatch without first having formulated the viewpoint defined by *general economy*.[25] There would be no potlatch if, in a general sense, the ultimate problem concerned the acquisition and not the dissipation of useful wealth.

The study of this strange yet familiar institution (a good many of our behaviors are reducible to the laws of potlatch; they have the same significance as it does) has a privileged place in general economy. If there is within us, running through the space we inhabit, a movement of energy that we use, but that is not reducible to its utility (which we are impelled by reason to seek), we can disregard it, but we can also adapt our activity to its completion outside us. The solution of the problem thus posed calls for an action in two contrary directions: We need on the one hand to go beyond the narrow limits within which we ordinarily remain, and on the other hand somehow bring our going-beyond back within our limits. The problem posed is that of the expenditure of the surplus. We need to give away, lose or destroy. But the gift would be senseless (and so we would never decide to give) if it did not take on the meaning of an acquisition. Hence *giving* must become *acquiring a power*. Gift-giving has the virtue of a surpassing of the subject who gives, but in exchange for the object given, the subject appropriates the surpassing: He regards his virtue, that which he had the capacity for, as an asset, as a *power* that he now possesses. He enriches himself with a contempt for riches, and what he proves to be miserly of is in fact his generosity.

But he would not be able by himself to acquire a power constituted by a relinquishment of power: If he destroyed the object in solitude, in silence, no sort of *power* would result from the act; there would not be anything for the subject but a separation from power without any compensation. But if he destroys the object in front of another person or if he gives it away, the one who gives has actually acquired, in the other's eyes, the power of giving or destroying. He is now rich for having made use of wealth in the manner its essence would require: He is rich for having ostentatiously consumed what is wealth only if it is consumed. But the wealth that is actualized in the potlatch, *in consumption for others,* has no real existence except insofar as the other is changed by the consumption. In a sense, authentic consumption ought to be solitary, but then it would not have the completion that the action it has on the other confers on it. And this action that is brought to bear on others is precisely what constitutes the gift's power, which one acquires from the fact of *losing*. The exemplary virtue of the potlatch is given in this possibility for man to grasp what eludes him, to combine the limitless movements of the universe with the limit that belongs to him.

2. *The apparent absurdity of gifts.*
But "you can't have your cake and eat it too," the saying goes.

It is contradictory to try to be unlimited and limited at the same time, and the result is comedy: The gift does not mean anything from the standpoint of general economy; there is dissipation only for the giver.

Moreover, it turns out that the giver has only apparently lost. Not only does he have the power over the recipient that the gift has bestowed on him, but the recipient is obligated to nullify that power by repaying the gift. The rivalry even entails the return of a greater gift: In order to *get even* the giver must not only redeem himself, but he must also impose the "power of the gift" on his rival in turn. In a sense the presents are repaid *with interest*. Thus the gift is the opposite of what it seemed to be: To give is obviously to lose, but the loss apparently brings a profit to the one who sustains it.

In reality, this absurdly contradictory aspect of potlatch is misleading. The first giver *suffers* the apparent gain resulting from the difference between his presents and those given to him in return. The one who repays only has the feeling of acquiring — a power — and of outdoing. Actually, as I have said, the ideal would be that a potlatch could not be repaid. The benefit in no way corresponds to the desire for gain. On the contrary, receiving prompts one — and obliges one — to give more, for it is necessary to remove the resulting obligation.

3. *The acquisition of rank.*
Doubtless potlatch is not reducible to the desire to lose, but what it brings to the giver is not the inevitable increase of return gifts; it is the rank *which it confers on the one who has the last word.*

Prestige, glory and rank should not be confused with *power*. Or if prestige is *power*, this is insofar as power itself escapes the considerations of force or right to which it is ordinarily reduced. It must be said, further, that the identity of the power and the ability to lose is fundamental. Numerous factors stand in the way, interfere and finally prevail, but, all things considered, neither force nor right is the *human basis* of the differentiated value of individuals. As the surviving practices make clear, *rank* varies decisively according to an individual's capacity for giving. The animal factor (the capacity for defeating an adversary in a fight) is itself subordinated, by and large, to the value of giving. To be sure, this is the ability to appropriate a position or possessions, but it is also the fact of a man's having staked his whole being. Moreover, the gift's aspect of an appeal to animal force is brought out in fights for a common cause, to which the fighter gives himself. *Glory*, the consequence of a superiority, is itself something different from an ability to take another's place and seize his possessions: It expresses a movement of senseless frenzy, of measureless expenditure of energy, which the fervor of combat presupposes. Combat is glorious in that it is always beyond calculation at some moment. But the meaning of warfare and glory is poorly grasped if it is not related in part to the acquisition of *rank* through a reckless expenditure of vital resources, of which potlatch is the most legible form.

4. *The first basic laws.*

But if it is true that potlatch remains the opposite of a rapine, of
a profitable exchange or, generally speaking, of an appropriation
of possessions, acquisition is nonetheless its ultimate purpose.
Because the movement it structures differs from ours, it appears
stranger to us, and so it is more capable of revealing what usually escapes our perception, and what it shows us is our basic
ambiguity. One can deduce the following laws from it. Of course
man is not definable once and for all and these laws operate differently — their effects are even neutralized — at different stages
of history, but basically they never cease to reveal a decisive play
of forces:

    • *a surplus of resources, which societies have constantly at their disposal
at certain points, at certain times, cannot be the object of a complete appropriation (it cannot be usefully employed; it cannot be employed for the
growth of the productive forces), but the squandering of this surplus itself
becomes an object of appropriation;*

    • *what is appropriated in the squander is the prestige it gives to the squan-
derer (whether an individual or a group), which is acquired by him as a
possession and which determines his* rank;

    • *conversely, rank in society (or the rank of one society among others)
can be appropriated in the same way as a tool or a field; if it is ultimately
a source of profit, the principle of it is nevertheless determined by a resolute squandering of resources that in theory could have been acquired.*

5. *Ambiguity and contradiction.*

While the resources he controls are reducible to quantities of energy, man is not always able to set them aside for a growth that cannot be endless or, above all, continual. He must waste the excess,
but he remains eager to acquire even when he does the opposite,
and so he makes waste itself an object of acquisition. Once the
resources are dissipated, there remains the prestige *acquired* by the

one who wastes. The waste is an ostentatious squandering to this end, with a view to a superiority over others that he attributes to himself by this means. But he misuses the negation he makes of the utility of the resources he wastes, bringing into contradiction not only himself but man's entire existence. The latter thus enters into an ambiguity where it remains: It places the value, the prestige and the truth of life in the negation of the servile use of possessions, but at the same time it makes a servile use of this negation. On the one hand, in the useful and graspable thing it discerns that which, being necessary to it, can be used for its growth (or its subsistence), but if strict necessity ceases to bind it, this "useful thing" cannot entirely answer to its wishes. Consequently, it calls for that which cannot be grasped, for the useless employment of oneself, of one's possessions, for *play*, but it attempts to grasp that which it wished to be *ungraspable*, to *use* that whose *utility* it denied. It is not enough for our left hand not to know what the right hand gives: Clumsily, it tries to take it back.

Rank is entirely the effect of this crooked will. In a sense, *rank* is the opposite of a thing: What founds it is sacred, and the general ordering of ranks is given the name of *hierarchy*. It is the stubborn determination to treat as a disposable and usable *thing* that whose essence is sacred, that which is completely removed from the profane utilitarian sphere, where the hand — unscrupulously and for servile ends — raises the hammer and nails the timber. But ambiguity encumbers the profane operation just as it empties desire's vehemence of its meaning and changes it into an apparent comedy.

This compromise given in our nature heralds those linked series of deceptions, exploitations and manias that give a temporal order to the apparent unreason of history. Man is necessarily in a mirage, his very reflection mystifies him, so intent is he on grasping the ungraspable, on using transports of lost hatred as tools. *Rank*, where loss is changed into acquisition, corresponds to the activity of the intellect, which reduces the objects of thought to *things*. In point of fact, the contradiction of potlatch is revealed not only throughout history, but more profoundly in the operations of thought. Generally, in sacrifice or in potlatch, in action (in history) or in contemplation (in thought), what we seek is always this semblance – which by definition we cannot grasp – that we vainly call the poetry, the depth or the intimacy of passion. We are necessarily deceived since we want to grasp this shadow.

We could not reach the final object of knowledge without the dissolution of knowledge, which aims to reduce its object to the condition of subordinated and managed things. The ultimate problem of knowledge is the same as that of consumption. No one can both know and not be destroyed; no one can both consume wealth and increase it.

6. *Luxury and extreme poverty.*
But if the demands of the life of beings (or groups) detached from life's immensity defines an interest to which every operation is referred, the *general* movement of life is nevertheless accomplished beyond the demands of individuals. Selfishness is finally disappointed. It seems to prevail and to lay down a definitive boundary, but it is surpassed in any case. No doubt the rivalries of individuals among themselves take away the multitude's ability to be overrun by the global exuberance of energy. The weak are fleeced, exploited by the strong, who pay them with flagrant lies. But this cannot change the overall results, where individual interest is mocked, and where *the lies of the rich are changed into truth*.

In the end, with the possibility of growth or of acquisition reaching its limit at a certain point, *energy*, the object of greed of every isolated individual, is necessarily liberated – truly liberated under the cover of lies. Definitively, men lie; they do their

best to relate this liberation to interest, but this liberation carries them further. Consequently, in a sense they lie in any case.
As a rule the individual accumulation of resources is doomed to
destruction. The individuals who carry out this destruction do
not truly possess this wealth, *this rank*. Under primitive conditions,
wealth is always analogous to stocks of munitions, which so clearly
express the annihilation, not the possession of wealth. But this
image is just as accurate if it is a matter of expressing the equally
ludicrous truth of *rank*: It is an explosive charge. The man of high
rank is originally only an explosive individual (all men are explosive, but he is explosive is a privileged way). Doubtless he tries
to prevent, or at least delay the explosion. Thus he lies to himself by derisively taking his wealth and his power for something
that they are not. If he manages to enjoy them peacefully, it is at
the cost of a misunderstanding of himself, of his real nature. He
lies at the same time to all the others, before whom on the contrary he maintains the affirmation of a truth (his explosive nature),
from which he tries to escape. Of course, he will be engulfed in
these lies: *Rank* will be reduced to a commodity of exploitation,
a shameless source of profits. This poverty cannot in any way inter-
rupt the movement of exuberance.

Indifferent to intentions, to reticences and lies, slowly or suddenly, the movement of wealth exudes and consumes the resources
of energy. This often seems strange, but not only do these resources
suffice; if they cannot be completely consumed productively a
surplus usually remains, which must be annihilated. At first sight,
potlatch appears to carry out this consumption badly. The destruction of riches is not its rule: They are ordinarily given away and
the loss in the operation is reduced to that of the giver: The aggregate of riches is preserved. But this is only an appearance. If potlatch rarely results in acts similar in every respect to sacrifice, it
is nonetheless *the complementary form of an institution whose mean-*

ing is in the fact that it withdraws wealth from productive consumption.
In general, sacrifice withdraws useful products from profane circulation; in principle the gifts of potlatch liberate objects that
are useless from the start. The industry of archaic luxury is the
basis of potlatch; obviously, this industry squanders resources represented by the quantities of available human labor. Among the
Aztecs, they were "cloaks, petticoats, precious blouses"; or "richly
coloured feathers...cut stones, shells, fans, shell paddles...wild-
animal skins worked and ornamented with designs." In the American Northwest, canoes and houses are destroyed, and dogs or slaves
are slaughtered: These are useful riches. Essentially the gifts are
objects of luxury (elsewhere the gifts of food are pledged from
the start to the useless consumption of feasts).

One might even say that potlatch is the specific manifestation,
the meaningful form of luxury. Beyond the archaic forms, luxury
has actually retained the functional value of potlatch, creative of
rank. Luxury still determines the rank of the one who displays
it, and there is no exalted rank that does not require a display.
But the petty calculations of those who enjoy luxury are surpassed
in every way. In wealth, what shines through the defects extends
the brilliance of the sun and provokes passion. It is not what is
imagined by those who have reduced it to their *poverty*; it is the
return of life's immensity to the truth of exuberance. This truth
destroys those who have taken it for what it is not; the least that
one can say is that the present forms of wealth make a shambles
and a human mockery of those who think they own it. In this
respect, present-day society is a huge counterfeit, where this *truth*
of wealth has underhandedly slipped into *extreme poverty*. The true
luxury and the real potlatch of our times falls to the poverty-
stricken, that is, to the individual who lies down and scoffs. A
genuine luxury requires the complete contempt for riches, the
somber indifference of the individual who refuses work and makes

76

his life on the one hand an infinitely ruined splendor, and on the other, a silent insult to the laborious lie of the rich. Beyond a military exploitation, a religious mystification and a capitalist misappropriation, henceforth no one can rediscover the meaning of wealth, the explosiveness that it heralds, unless it is in the splendor of rags and the somber challenge of indifference. One might say, finally, that the lie destines life's exuberance to revolt.

PART THREE

The Historical Data II

The Society of
Military Enterprise and the
Society of
Religious Enterprise

The Conquering Society: Islam

The Difficulty of Giving a Meaning
to the Moslem Religion

Islam, the religion of Mohammed, is, together with Buddhism
and Christianity, one of the three world religions. It takes in a
substantial portion of the population of the globe, and provided
the faithful fulfills specific moral obligations in his lifetime,
it promises beatitude after death. Like Christianity, it affirms
the existence of a single God, but it is adamant concerning his
unicity: It regards the dogma of the Trinity as an abomination.
The Moslem only recognizes one God, of whom Mohammed is
the messenger, but Mohammed has no access to God's divinity.
He is not like Jesus, who partakes of both man and God, a me-
diator between two worlds. There is no attenuation of Islam's
divine transcendence: Mohammed is only a man, honored by a
decisive revelation.

In theory these tenets adequately define Islam. We shall add
to them the recognition, on a secondary plane, of the Judeo-
Christian tradition (Moslems speak of Abraham and of Jesus, but
the latter is only a prophet himself). There remains the rather well-
known history of Mohammed's disciples: the conquests of the first
caliphs, the dislocation of the empire, the successive invasions

of the Mongols and the Turks, followed by the decline of the Moslem powers in our time.

All this is clear, but only superficially so. If we try to enter into the spirit that determined a vast movement and ordered the lives of countless multitudes over centuries, we do not see what could have touched us personally, but only formal particulars, whose attraction for the faithful we can only sense by imagining the local color of costumes, of strange cities, and a whole series of hieratic attitudes and gestures. Mohammed himself, whose life is well known to us, speaks a language that does not have the clear and irreplaceable meaning for us that Buddha's or Christ's has. If only we are alert, Buddha or Christ speak to us, but Mohammed to others.

So true is the above that whenever the undeniable seduction that we feel tries to express itself in words, we don't know what to say. The principles then appear as they are: foreign to what affects us. We can only resort to platitudes.

One cannot doubt the sincerity or the competence of Emile Dermenghem where, at the conclusion of the rich volume which the *Cahiers du Sud* has recently devoted to Islam, he outlines the values that Islam conveys to us.[1] It is no use blaming anything but an irreducible difficulty. But the fact that the emphasis is placed on freedom as against servitude, on gentleness as against violence, is surprising, and indicative of the perplexity of some- one trying to formulate a deep attraction. When Dermenghem speaks of freedom he is expressing the attraction he feels both to freedom and to Islam, but the quotations he offers are uncon- vincing.[2] "God does not love oppressors," says the Koran. One grants the antithesis of the idea of God and an unjust oppression, but this is not a Moslem trait. And one cannot fail to note the generally despotic nature of sovereignty in Islam. Is freedom not based on revolt, and is it not the same thing as unsubmissiveness?

Now the very word, *islam*, means submission. A Moslem is someone who submits.[3] He submits to God, to the discipline that God
demands, which is consistent with that demanded by his lieuten-
ants: Islam is discipline as opposed to the capricious virility, the
individualism of the Arabs of the polytheistic tribes. Nothing is
more contrary to the ideas that the virile word *freedom* evokes
in our minds.

A passage on war is no less strange.[4] Dermenghem is doubtless right to underscore the fact that for Mohammed the great *holy
war* is not that of the Moslem against the infidel but that of the
renunciation one must engage in against oneself. He is also right
to illustrate the moderate character of Islam by reference to the
humanity shown in its first conquests. But if one speaks "of war"
apropos of the Moslems in order to praise them, it is best not to
separate this moderation from their principles. In their eyes, every
violent action against infidels is good. From the first period, at
Medina, the disciples of Mohammed lived by pillaging. "On the
occasion of a Moslem raid," says Maurice Gaudefroy-Demombynes,
"the Koran (II, 212) told the Moslems to fight even though the
raid was carried out in violation of the truce of the pre-Islamic
sacred months."[5]

The *hadith* (the written tradition and a kind of code of ancient
Islam) organized the conquest systematically. It excluded needless exactions and acts of violence. The regimen imposed on those
defeated persons who came to terms with the victor had to be
humane, especially if it was a question of men of Scripture (Chris-
tians, Jews and Zoroastrians). These were only subjected to tax-
ation. Likewise the *hadith* ordained that the crops, trees, and
irrigation works should be respected.[6] But

> the imam of the Moslem community must wage *jihad* (holy
> war) against the peoples of the "war territory" immediately

adjacent to the "territory of Islam." The leaders of the army must make sure that these peoples know the teachings of Islam and that they refuse to follow them: it is then necessary to fight them. The holy war was permanent, therefore, at the borders of Islam. There was no real peace possible between Moslems and infidels. This was an absolute theoretical notion that could not hold up against the facts, and the juridical expedient had to be found, the *hila*, for circumventing it while conforming to it. The doctrine granted that the Moslem princes might enter into truces with the infidels, lasting ten years at the most, in the case of an insurmountable weakness of the Moslem state and in the latter's interest. They were free to break them at will, provided they atoned for their violated oath.[7]

How could one fail to see a means of expansion, of indefinite growth, in these precepts, one that is perfect at the same time in its principle, in its effects and in the duration of its effects?

Some of Dermenghem's other views are also in the nature of vague approximations. But this clear question emerges: How does one grasp the meaning of an institution that has outlived its reason for being? Islam is a discipline applied to a methodical effort of conquest. The completed enterprise is an empty framework; thus the moral riches Islam holds are those of mankind in general, but its external consequences are more marked, less unstable and more formal.

The Arab Societies of Consumption Before the Hegira

If we are to define the meaning of the Prophet's discipline, of Islam, we cannot leave off at its survival, which in our view preserves the beauty of death or of ruins. Islam opposes to the Arab world where it was born the determination that made an empire out of elements that were scattered until then. We are relatively well informed about the small Arab communities, no larger than the tribe, which had a difficult existence before the Hegira. They were not always nomadic, but the difference between the nomads and the sedentary inhabitants of the poor villages – such as Mecca or Yatrib (the future Medina) – was relatively slight. Within the confines of harsh tribal rules they maintained a stormy individualism to which the importance of their poetry is connected. The personal or tribal rivalries, the bouts of bravura, of gallantry, of prodigality, of eloquence, of poetic talent, played the greatest role in them. Ostentatious giving and squandering were rampant and one can doubtless infer the existence of a ritual form of potlatch from a prescription of the Koran: "Do not give in order to have more" (LXXIV, 6). Having remained polytheistic, many of these tribes had bloody sacrifices (others were Christian or Jewish, but then it was the tribe, and not the individual, which had chosen the religion and it is doubtful that the way of life was changed very much as a result). Blood vengeance, the obligation for the relatives of a man killed to take their revenge on the killer's relatives, completed this tableau of wasteful acts of violence.

Assuming that the neighboring regions, endowed with a strong military organization, were closed to the possibility of expansion, this spendthrift way of life could ensure a lasting equilibrium (the frequent killing of the female newborn helped to prevent overpopulation). But if the neighbors had weakened, the maintenance of a way of life that did not provide for a joining of forces would not have allowed these people to take advantage of the fact. A preliminary reformation of customs, the formulation of a preliminary principle of conquest, of enterprise and of unification of forces, were necessary before any aggression could be undertaken, even against states in decline. Apparently Mohammed did not mean to respond to the possibilities that resulted from the weakness of the neighboring states, but his teaching nonetheless had the same effect as it would have had if he had clearly intended to profit from the occasion.

Properly speaking, these pre-Islamic Arabs had not reached the stage of military enterprise any more than the Aztecs had. These ways of life correspond to the principle of a society of consumption. But among people of the same stage, the Aztecs had exercised a military hegemony. The Arabs, whose neighbors were Sassanid Iran and Byzantium, were forced to vegetate.

Nascent Islam or Society Reduced to Military Enterprise

"The pietism of primitive Islam," writes H. Holma, "would certainly deserve to be studied and examined more closely, especially since Max Weber and Sombart have clearly shown the importance of the pietist way of thinking in the origins and development of capitalism."[8] This remark by the Finnish writer is all the more pertinent since the pietism of the Jews and the Protestants was motivated by intentions alien to capitalism. It nevertheless resulted in the birth of an economy in which the accumulation of capital dominated (to the detriment of consumption, which was the rule in the Middle Ages).[9] In any case, Mohammed could not have done any better if he had set out to transform the reckless and wasteful agitation of the Arabs of his time into an effective instrument of conquest.

The action of Moslem puritanism is comparable to that of the manager of a factory in which disorder has taken hold: He takes wise measures to fill the gaps in the plant that have drained off the energy and reduced the output to nothing. Mohammed opposed the *muruwa*, the glorious and individual "ideal" of virility of the pre-Islamic tribes, with the *din*, with faith and submissive discipline. (Richelieu combatting the traditions of feudal honor, the duel, chose this same direction deliberately.) He forbade blood

86

vengeance within the Moslem community, but allowed it against infidels. He condemned the killing of infants, the use of wine and the gift of rivalry. He replaced this gift-giving for the sake of pure vainglory with the socially useful giving of alms. "Render your close relative his due, as well as the pauper and the wayfarer. Yet do not squander extravagantly; spendthrifts are the devil's brethren" (Koran, XVII, 28-29). Extreme generosity, a major virtue of the tribes, suddenly became an object of aversion, and individual pride was condemned. The squandering, intractable and savage warrior, lover and beloved of young women, hero of the tribes' poetry, gives way to the devout soldier, the formal observer of discipline and rites. The custom of praying in common was a constant external affirmation of this change; it has rightly been compared to military exercise, which unifies and mechanizes hearts. The contrast of the Koran (and the *hadith*) with the capricious world of poetry symbolizes this repudiation. It was only after the irresistible wave of conquest by the devout army that the tradition was resumed: Victorious Islam was not held to the same severity; generous squander, for which the longing remained, ceased to be a danger once the empire had consolidated its domination.

The alternation of austerity, which accumulates, with prodigality, which dissipates, is the ordinary rhythm in the use of energy. Only relative austerity and the absence of dissipation allow for the growth of the energy systems that living beings or societies constitute. But, at least for a time, growth has its limits and it is necessary to dissipate the excess that cannot be accumulated. What gives Islam a place apart in these movements is the fact that it was open from the start to an apparently unlimited increase of power. This was by no means a consistent plan or project, but chance realized every possibility. And chance was supported by a minimum of necessity. It is relatively easy to assemble people by inspiring them with a particular enthusiasm. But one must give

them something to *do*. To assemble, to exalt is first of all to elicit
an unapplied force; this force cannot follow its impetus and press
forward unless it is used the moment it becomes available. From
the first, Islam was fortunate in having to set itself violently against
the world in which it originated. Mohammed's teaching opposed
it to the tribe whose traditions it blasphemed. The tribe threatened to exclude it, which was equivalent to death. It thus had
to repudiate the tribal relationship, and since an existence without ties was not conceivable at the time, it had to establish a different type of bond between it and its adherents. This was the
meaning of the Hegira, which properly began the Moslem era:
Mohammed's flight from Mecca to Medina consecrated the rup-
ture of blood ties and the establishment of a new community based
on chosen brotherhood, open to anyone who adopted its religious
forms. Christianity dates from the individual birth of a redeeming
god; Islam, from the birth of a community, of a new kind of state,
which did not have its basis in either blood or place. Islam differs
from Christianity and Buddhism in that it became, after the Hegira,
something different from a teaching propagated in the framework
of a society already formed (a local or blood community). It was
the establishment of a society based on the new teaching.

This principle was in a sense perfect. There was no room for
ambiguity or compromise: The religious leader was at the same
time the legislator, the judge and the military chief. One cannot
imagine a more rigorously unified community. The social bond
had its origin in will alone (but will could not break it), which
offered the advantage not only of ensuring a deep moral unity,
but also of opening Islam to indefinite expansion.

It was an admirable machinery. Military order replaced the anarchy of rival clans, and individual resources, no longer consumed
wastefully, went into the service of the armed community. Once
the obstacle (the tribal boundary) that formerly stood in the way

of growth had been removed, the individual forces were kept in store for military campaigns. Conquest, which the *hadith* methodically fashioned into a means of expansion, invested the new resources, without appreciable destruction, in a closed system of forces that grew larger and larger at a faster and faster rate. This movement recalls the development of industry through capitalist accumulation: If waste is halted, if development no longer has a formal limit, the afflux of energy dictates growth, and growth multiplies the accumulation.

So uncommon a perfection is not without its other side, however. If one compares the Moslem conquests with the development of the Christian or Buddhist religion, one soon notes the relative powerlessness of Islam. The fact is that the formation of power demands that one forego its use. The development of industry requires a limit on consumption: Equipment gets first priority; immediate interest is subordinated to it. The very principle of Islam implied the same order of values: Life loses its immediate power of disposal to the pursuit of a greater power. In avoiding the moral weakness of the Christian and Buddhist communities (forced to serve an unchanged political system), Islam fell into a greater weakness, the consequence of a complete subordination of religious life to military necessity. The pious Moslem renounced not only the wasteful expenditures of the tribal world but also, as a general rule, any expenditure of force that was not an external violence turned against the infidel enemy. The internal violence that founds a religious life and culminates in a sacrifice played only a secondary role in the Islam of the first period. For Islam is defined not by consumption but, like capitalism, by an accumulation of available forces. In its primary essence, Islam is unamenable to any dramatization, to any transfixed contemplation of drama. There is nothing in it corresponding to Christ's death on the cross, or to Buddha's rapture of annihilation. Like the military sovereign who unleashes his violence against the enemy, it sets itself against the religious sovereign, who undergoes violence. The military sovereign is never killed and even tends to put an end to sacrifices; he is there to direct the violence outside, and to preserve the vital force of the community from internal consumption, from ruination. He is committed from the start to the path of appropriations, of conquests, of calculated expenditures, whose purpose is growth. Islam is in a sense, in its unity, a synthesis of religious and military forms; it has curtailed sacrifices, limiting religion to morality, alms-giving and prayer observance.

Late Islam or the Return to Stability

Given its foundation and its conquests, the meaning of Islam gets lost in the constituted Moslem empire. As soon as Islam ceased, because of its victories, to be a rigorous devotion of vital forces to growth, it remained nothing but an empty, rigid framework. What came to it from elsewhere was not taken into this rigorous cohesion without being transformed. But except for the cohesion, there is nothing in it that was not given before it. It quickly opened itself to the influence of the conquered lands whose riches it inherited.

It is more than a little strange that once the conquests were consolidated the underlying Arab civilization, the negation of which had been a founding principle, recovered its vitality and continued much as before. Something of that *muruwa* of the tribes, to which Mohammed opposed the rigors of the Koran, subsisted in the Arab world, which maintained a tradition of chivalrous values in which violence was combined with prodigality, and love with poetry. Moreover, what we ourselves have from Islam does not partake of Mohammed's contribution, but precisely of those condemned values. It is curious to recognize an Arab influence in our chivalrous "religion," so different from the institution of chivalry revealed in the *chansons de geste*, the latter being quite foreign to the Moslem world. The very expression, *chivalrous*, took on a new meaning during the time of the Crusades, a poetic meaning tied to the value of passion. In the twelfth century, in the West, the ordinary interpretation of the ritual of armament was Moslem. And the birth, in the South of France, of the poetry of passion apparently extended a tradition going back, via Andalusia, to those poetry competitions of the tribes that provoked the austere reaction of the Prophet.[10]

The Unarmed Society: Lamaism

The Peaceful Societies

In a sense, Islam differs from ordinary societies of military enterprise by an exaggeration of traits. One sees tendencies in it, carried to extremes, that are less pronounced in the imperial ventures
of classical antiquity or China. True, one does not find the birth
of a morality in connection with Islam: It adopted a morality that
pre-existed it. But the clear break it made with the society out
of which it came gives to the figure it formed the sharpness that
the more ancient empires do not have. Indeed, the subordination
of conquest to morality is what specifies, and abridges, its meaning.

It is paradoxical, perhaps, to have chosen it, in preference to
the more classical Rome or China, to illustrate a type of civilization. And it is strange to bring forward Lamaism, instead of the
Christian Church, to describe an unarmed society. But the contrast is clearer, the play of elements is more intelligible when one
gives extreme examples.

In a humanity everywhere prepared to start a war, Tibet is paradoxically an enclave of peaceful civilization, incapable of attacking
others or defending itself. Poverty, immensity, topography and cold
are in this case the only defenders of a country with no military
force. The population, little different racially from the Huns and

the Mongols (in times past, moreover, the Tibetans would invade China, exacting tributes from the emperors), at the beginning of the twentieth century proved incapable of fighting militarily, incapable of offering more than a day's resistance to two successive invasions, by the British (1904) and by the Chinese (1909). It is true that an insurmountable inferiority in weaponry made a defeat of the invaders unlikely. Yet other poorly equipped armies elsewhere effectively opposed even armored forces. And Tibet has the advantage of an all but inaccessible position. In reality a positive determination is involved. The Nepalese, whose race, location and material culture are quite similar, have on the contrary a large military capability (they even invaded Tibet various times).

At first sight, it is easy to give a reason for this peaceableness: Its origin is Buddhism, which forbids its adherents to kill. Warlike Nepal is dominated politically by the Hindu military aristocracy of the Gurkhas. But the Buddhist Tibetans are very pious: Their sovereign is a high dignitary of the clergy. The explanation is not so clear, however. In spite of everything, a feeble reaction in the face of an invasion is bizarre. Other religions condemn war, and the people who profess them obviously still manage to kill one another. One would like to look more closely at things, and the posthumous work of a British official, Sir Charles Bell, devoted both to the personal life of the thirteenth Dalai Lama (1876-1934) and to the history of Tibet under his reign, enables one to follow the *material operation of the system* rather well.[11]

Modern Tibet and its British Annalist

This book by Charles Bell is better than a biography or a history. It is not a composed work but a first-hand document, the disorganized chronicle of a witness involved in events, relating what happens to him as he goes along. The author gives a brief account of things he has not experienced directly, but he dwells more at length on the small occurrences of his own life: He does not spare us the least detail concerning his stay in Tibet, or in India, where he was in contact with the Dalai Lama. The work is poorly done, but it is more lively and offers more than a formal study; it is a jumble, but no matter: We do not have a less systematic or more complete document on the civilization of Tibet. Charles Bell is the first white man to have had sustained relations, based on a kind of friendship, with a Dalai Lama. This very honorable diplomatic agent appears to have felt a genuine concern not only for the interests of his own country but for those of Tibet, whose language he knew. Even the government of India, not very anxious to get involved, seems to have called on his services with a certain amount of hesitation. Charles Bell thought that the British should help the Tibetans to maintain their independence, to throw off the Chinese yoke for good. The British finally did adopt this policy, which was intended to make Tibet a zone of influence, but in a cautious way. They saw the advantage of a buffer state and they were very much in favor of a strong, autonomous Tibet, but a rampart against eventual difficulties must not be gained at the cost of serious immediate difficulties. They wanted to avoid having the Chinese as neighbors, but not if this meant supporting hostilities against them.

A period of Anglo-Tibetan friendship, rather warm around 1920, at least enabled the author to reside at leisure and take political initiatives in a country that had remained closed to whites for more than a century. And while the institutions of Tibet were not unknown prior to Bell, certainly, one could not grasp its life and vicissitudes from within. We do not enter a system until we can perceive its fluctuations, until we discover an interaction of its elements in operation. Charles Bell, during a year's stay at Lhasa, tried to engage the government of Tibet in a military policy. Couldn't Tibet have an army in proportion to its means? It so happens that the difficulties he encountered enable us to examine an economic paradox. From this paradox, the various possibilities of human society and the general conditions of an equilibrium emerge in clearer relief.

The Purely Religious Power of the Dalai Lama

The special aim of the last book by Charles Bell (who died in 1950) is the biography of the thirteenth Dalai Lama. This objective naturally led him to review the known origins of an institution that has no strict counterpart other than the papacy. I will summarize these historical facts. Buddhism was introduced into Tibet in 640. Tibet was then governed by kings, and in the first period the development of this religion did not at all weaken the country, which was one of the chief military powers of Asia. But Buddhist monasticism spread and in the course of time the influence of the monasteries threatened that of the kings. In the twelfth century a reformer, Tsong-Ka-Pa, founded a more severe sect, in which the monks observed strict celibacy. The reformed sect of the "Yellow Hats" opposed the looser sect of the "Red Hats." A saintly, or even divine character was attributed to the "Yellow Hats," which, reappearing in their successors, gave them the spiritual power and religious sovereignty. One of them, a great lama of the "Rice Heap" monastery near Lhasa, allied himself with a Mongol chief who defeated a last "Red Hat" king. In this way Tibet came under the authority of the "Dalai Lama," a mongol title given on this occasion to the fifth incarnation of that superhuman personage.

This Dalai Lama was not clearly the most important of the incarnate gods of Tibet. The semi-legendary narratives that deal with the origins in a sense give higher standing to the "Panchen" of Ta-shi Lün-po (a monastery west of Lhasa). In reality the spiritual authority of the Dalai Lama grew out of his temporal authority. The Panchen himself has, in addition to an immense religious prestige, secular charge of a province; he has his own policy as an unsubmissive vassal. The same is true, to lesser degrees, of other great lamas, since an important monastery is a fief in a barely centralized kingdom, like a state within a state. But the sovereignty of the Dalai Lama achieved consistency in that it ceased to be linked to the function that established it. In our time, the head of government of Tibet is so little the grand lama of the "Rice Heap" that this monastery, rebellious at times, could conduct a pro-Chinese policy and thwart the pro-British policy of Lhasa.

This indecisive character of the local institutions is reflected in Tibet's relations with China. The authority of the Dalai Lama, which is not based on any military power, has never exercised more than a fragile control over the play of forces to which it could not offer any real obstacle. A sovereignty is precarious that does not command both the religious enthrallment of the people and the half-mercenary, half-emotional obedience of an army. And in fact theocratic Tibet soon fell under the dominion of China. The origin of this vassalage is not clear. The Tibetans dispute the Chinese version; the Chinese, the Tibetan one. Tibet was often subjected to Chinese rule even in antiquity, but not like a fief subjected to a suzerain (by a traditional right recognized by both parties): It was a matter of force, and force quickly overturned what force had established. China intervened in Tibet as far back as the seventeenth century, doing what it could to control the selection of the Dalai Lamas. An amban, backed by a garrison, had the real secular power. Generally speaking, the garrison seems to have been weak; Tibet was not a protectorate (there was no colonization, the administration remaining entirely Tibetan). But China had the upper hand and owing to its agents the sovereignty of the Dalai Lama was fictitious: It may have been divine, but it was also powerless.

It was all the easier to nullify the Dalai Lama's power since a bizarre mode of succession periodically abandoned the country to regents for long intervals. In the eyes of the Tibetans the Dalai Lama is no mortal, or rather, he dies only in appearance and is soon reincarnated. He was regarded from the beginning as the incarnation of a mythical being, Chen-re-zi, protector and god of Tibet in the Buddhist pantheon. The general reincarnation of human beings (in other animal or human creatures) after death is the object of a fundamental belief for Buddhists. Thus on the death of a Dalai Lama, always attributed to the *desire* to die, it is necessary to go in search of a male child, in whose body he is soon reborn. An official oracle designates the province and inquiries are conducted concerning children born within a period of time corresponding to the death of the late Dalai Lama. The decisive sign is the recognition of an object that was used in the previous incarnation: The child must choose it from among other similar objects. The young Dalai Lama, discovered at the age of four years, is then introduced and enthroned, but he does not exercise power before his nineteenth year. Thus, taking account of the time lapse for reincarnation, a 20-year regency must separate two reigns. Moreover, this regency is often prolonged. It suffices for the young sovereign to die young. As a matter of fact, the four Dalai Lamas prior to the thirteenth died before or shortly after the assumption of power, a development in which the interests of the Chinese "ambans" are thought to have had a part. A regent is more manageable and, moreover, has some interest himself in resorting to poison.

The Powerlessness and Revolt of the Thirteenth Dalai Lama

By way of an exception, the thirteenth Dalai Lama survived. This was perhaps due to a noticeable decline of the Chinese influence. The amban had already stayed out of things at the time of the

child's selection. This new god was born in 1876; he was invested
with full powers, religious and secular, in 1895. Tibet was not then
better armed than before, but it was generally defended by an
extreme difficulty of access. The de facto power of the Dalai Lama
is always possible at the first easing of attention on the part of
the Chinese, but it is then completely precarious. The young sovereign learned this quickly, despite the ignorance in which he was
kept by his isolation from everything and his upbringing as an idol,
as a monk lost in meditation. He made a first mistake. A letter
from the viceroy of India asked for the opening of the Tibetan
markets to Hindus: The Dalai Lama returned it unopened. The
matter was not very significant in itself, but the British could not
bear being next to a country that was closed to them, that risked
being opened to Russian influence or even, it was said, handed
over to Russia by the Chinese. The government of India sent a
political mission charged with establishing satisfactory relations
with Lhasa. The Tibetans opposed the entry of envoys into their
territory. In this way the mission became military: At the head
of a detachment, Colonel Younghusband broke the resistance and
marched on Lhasa. The Chinese did not budge; the Dalai Lama
fled, but not before placing the governmental seal in the hands
of a monk recognized for his saintliness and learning. The only
conditions the British imposed on leaving Lhasa were the opening of three Tibetan towns to commerce, recognition of their protectorate over a border province, Sikkim, and lastly, no other
foreign power was to intervene in Tibet. This treaty defined a zone
of British influence, but it also implicitly recognized Tibet's sovereignty; it ignored the Chinese suzerainty. The Chinese put up
notices in some towns of Tibet, proclaiming the deposing of the
Dalai Lama, but the populace covered these papers with manure.
The Dalai Lama stayed four years in China, going from Mongolia
to Shansi, then to Peking. The relations of the living Buddha with

the Son of the Heavens remained ambiguous (the Chinese seemed to forget about the dethronement) and strained during this time. Rather abruptly, the Dalai Lama set out on the return journey to Tibet. But the day he arrived in Lhasa he had at his heels a Chinese army, instructed to kill his ministers and lock him up in a temple. He resumed the road of exile, this time toward the south. In the dead of winter, passing through snowstorms on horseback, exhausted, he and his party reached a border post and requested the protection of two British telegraph operators whom he had directed to be awakened in the night. In this way he demonstrated that the most firmly established religious power is at the mercy of a real power based on armed force. He could only base himself on fatigue, or at best on the prudence of the neighboring countries. The British gladly welcomed this fugitive who had been unable to govern but without whom authority was useless. For his part the Dalai Lama, instructed by bitter experience, saw the advantage he could derive from an antagonism between British India and China. But he overestimated it. The sovereign authority and mutual antagonism of neighbors are useful to a state's autonomy but they alone cannot ensure it. The solicited British failed to satisfy the anxious expectations of the exiled leader. They refused their support, amicably limiting themselves to expressing their desire to see one day a strong Tibet, released from the Chinese yoke. The situation was finally reversed only by the internal difficulties of China (the fall of the Empire in 1911). The Tibetans drove out of Lhasa a garrison whose leaders no longer had any authority. The amban and the commander of the Chinese forces surrendered. The Dalai Lama re-entered the capital and returned to power after an exile of seven years. He managed very skillfully to stay in power until his death in 1934.

What distinguished this thirteenth Dalai Lama is that having survived, he acquired the experience of power — though under the most adverse conditions. There was no tradition that could have guided him. His teachers had given him a monk's education; he had learned little beyond the captivating and peaceful lamaic meditation, which is structured by meticulous speculation and a deep mythology and metaphysics. The studies pursued in the Tibetan lamaseries are quite demanding and the monks excel at difficult debate. But one would expect that such an education would be more apt to anesthetize than to arouse a feeling for the political necessities, especially in this part of the world that is inaccessible and deliberately closed to the outside. And especially at a time when the only foreigners allowed into Tibet were Chinese having neither the desire nor the possibility of informing.

Slowly, but steadily and sagaciously, the thirteenth Dalai Lama discovered the world. He turned his years of exile to account, never missing an opportunity to acquire knowledge useful to the conduct of the government. During a visit to Calcutta he became acquainted with the resources of advanced civilizations. Thus he ceased to be ignorant of the rest of a world in which he was to play his part. Through him Tibet became aware of the external play of forces, which could not be ignored or denied with impunity. More exactly, the religious and divine force that he constituted recognized its limits – and recognized that without a military force it could do nothing. His power was so clearly limited to internal sovereignty, to control over sacred ceremonies and silent meditations, that he rather naively offered the British the responsibility for external sovereignty and decision-making power over Tibet's foreign relations. They only had to continue to stay out of its internal affairs. (Bhutan accepted and approved these conditions, but that little country of northern India is a state whose affairs are of little consequence.) The British did not examine the proposal: They did not want any other influence in Tibet than their own, but they wanted rights limiting those of others, and

not a burden of responsibility. Almost without assistance and without force, the Dalai Lama thus had to face the rest of the world
and the task was heavy for him to bear.

No one can serve two masters. Tibet in its time had chosen
the monks: It had neglected the kings. All the prestige had gone
to lamas surrounded by legends and divine rituals. This system
had resulted in the abandonment of military force. Or rather military power had died: The fact that a lama carried the prestige of
a king took away the latter's ability to resist the pressure from
without. He had ceased to have the force of attraction necessary
to assemble an army for that purpose. But given this state of affairs,
the sovereign who had succeeded him had only done so outwardly:
He had not inherited that military power which he had destroyed.
The world of prayers had prevailed over that of arms, but it had
destroyed without acquiring force. In order to conquer, it had been
obliged to appeal to foreign intervention. And it had remained
at the mercy of outside forces, since it had destroyed that which
resisted within.

Those accidental relaxations (quickly followed by resumptions)
of outside pressure, which enabled the thirteenth Dali Lama to
endure, in the end only offered him proof of his powerlessness.
Being what he was, he really did not have the means to sustain
his status. Perhaps destiny had not been so unkind to the ninth,
tenth, eleventh and twelfth Dali Lamas, killed when they came
of age. And the apparent luck of the thirteenth was perhaps his
misfortune. The thirteenth accepted it scrupulously nevertheless;
he scrupulously accepted the responsibility of a *power* that *could
not* be exercised, that was essentially open to the outside and that
could expect nothing from the outside but death. So he resolved
to renounce his own essential being.

The Revolt of the Monks Against an Attempt at Military Organization

With the help of a respite (in China fatigue, then revolution), that had enabled him first to endure and then to overcome, the Dalai Lama arrived at the idea of restoring to Tibet the power that Lamaism had denied it. He was assisted in this task by the advice of his English biographer. Charles Bell, as the political agent of the government of India, did finally commit England to a friendly policy. Direct military aid continued to be refused; not even shipments of arms were considered, but during a year's official mission Charles Bell, "in his own name," supported the Dalai Lama in an effort aimed at military organization. It involved increasing the army gradually — in 20 years — from 6 thousand men to 17 thousand! A tax on the secular and monastic properties would cover the costs of the operation. The Dalai Lama's authority obliged the notables to acquiesce. But if it is easy *personally* to renounce, if it is possible to involve ministers and dignitaries, one cannot all of a sudden deprive a society of its essence.

Not only the majority of monks but the people were also affected. Increasing the army, even slightly, would diminish the importance of the monks. Now, there are no words of rites, there is no festival, no consciousness — in short, there is no human life in that country which does not depend on them. Everything else revolves around them. If someone, against all likelihood, were to turn away from the religion, he would still derive his meaning and his possibility of expression from the monks. The emergence of a new element, which was not content with surviving, *which grew*, could not be justified to the people by any other voice but theirs. To such an extent was the meaning of an action or a possibility given by and for the monks that the army's few supporters portrayed it as the only means of maintaining the religion. In 1909 the Chinese had burned the monasteries, killed the

monks and destroyed the holy books. But Tibet was in essence
the same thing as the monasteries. What good was it, people
said, to fight to uphold a principle if fighting meant abandoning
the principle in the first place? An important lama explained it
to Charles Bell: "It is of no use increasing the army in Tibet, for
it is written in 'the books' that Tibet will be conquered by foreigners from time to time, but they will not stay long." Even the
concern that the monks had for keeping their position, which
made them oppose the maintenance of an army (that would have
combated foreign invaders), caused them to fight on another
level. The winter of 1920–1921 was heavy with threats of riots
and civil war. One night, placards urging the people to kill Bell
were put up at various public places in Lhasa. February 22 began
the festival of the Great Prayer, which drew to Lhasa a gathering
of 50 to 60 thousand monks. A part of this crowd went through
the city shouting: "Come out and fight. We are not afraid to
give our lives." The festival unfolded in an atmosphere of tension.
The army's supporters and Bell himself attended fairy-like ceremonies and mingled with the populace in the streets, present-
ing a bold front to the storm, at the mercy of an excitation that
might have taken shape and direction at any moment. There
followed a rather moderate purge — remarkably moderate in
fact — and the rebellion lasted a long time. The military policy
of the Dalai Lama was prudent: It was based on elementary common sense, and the general hostility could offer nothing honorable against it. The monks' cause went in the direction of
betrayal, not only of Tibet, but of monasticism itself. It came
up against the firmness of an internally strong government; it was
lost from the start. And the surprising thing is not its failure, but
the fact that a first mass movement supported it so ardently. The
paradox is such that one is compelled to look for deeper reasons
behind it.

The Consumption of the Total Surplus by the Lamas

I will begin by setting aside the superficial explanation. Charles Bell stresses the fact that the Buddhist religion prohibits violence and condemns war. But other religions have these principles and one knows what the commandments of a church are worth in practice. A social behavior cannot result from a moral rule; it expresses the structure of a society, a play of material forces that animates it. What evidently commanded this movement of hostility was not a moral scruple, but rather — in a ponderous way — the self-interest of the monks. Moreover, this element is far from escaping the attention of Charles Bell, who contributes valuable information on the subject. One was aware of the extent of Lamaism before him: a monk for every three adult males, monasteries that numbered 7 to 8 thousand monks at any one time, a total of 250 to 500 thousand religious persons out of a population of 4 to 5 million. But the material significance of monasticism is specified by Charles Bell in budgetary terms.

According to him, the total revenue of the government of Lhasa in 1917 (the value of benefits in goods and services added to that of the currency) was approximately £720,000 yearly. Of that amount, the budget of the army was £150,000. That of the administration was £400,000. Of the remainder, an appreciable share was set aside by the Dalai Lama for the religious expenditures of the government. But in addition to these governmental expenditures, Bell estimates that the revenue spent yearly by the clergy (income from the property holdings of the monasteries, gifts and payments of religious services) was well over £1,000,000. *Thus in theory the total budget of the Church would have been twice as large as that of the state, eight times that of the army.*

These figures based on a personal assessment have no official character. But they nevertheless illuminate the reason for the opposition encountered by the military policy. If a nation dedicates its vital forces, almost unreservedly, to monastic organization, it cannot at the same time have an army. Elsewhere no doubt a sharing is possible between religious and military life. But what the budgetary facts end up showing is precisely an exclusive dedication. The creation of an army may have been rationally called for, but it was nonetheless at odds with the feeling on which life was founded; it nonetheless introduced a malaise into the country. To go back on so absolute a decision would have been to renounce oneself; it would have been like drowning in order to escape the rain. One still needs to say how this feeling took hold in the beginning; one still needs to show the deep reason that, once upon a time, caused a whole country to become a monastery, that, in the midst of a real world, finally caused this country, an integral part of that world, to opt out of it.

The Economic Explanation of Lamaism

One would not arrive at the real cause in this instance if one did not first perceive the general law of economy: On the whole a society always produces more than is necessary for its survival; it has a surplus at its disposal. It is precisely the use it makes of this surplus that determines it: The surplus is the cause of the agitation, of the structural changes and of the entire history of society. But the surplus has more than one outlet, the most common of which is growth. And growth itself has many forms, each one of which eventually comes up against some limit. Thwarted, demographic growth becomes military; it is forced to engage in conquest. Once the military limit is reached, the surplus has the sumptuary forms of religion as an outlet, along with the games and spectacles that derive therefrom, or personal luxury.

History ceaselessly records the cessation, then the resumption of growth. There are states of equilibrium where the increased sumptuary life and the reduced bellicose activity give the excess

its most humane outlet. But this state itself dissolves society little by little, and returns it to disequilibrium. Some new movement then appears as the only bearable solution. Under these
conditions of malaise, a society engages as soon as it can in an
undertaking capable of increasing its forces. It is then ready to
recast its moral laws; it uses the surplus for new ends, which suddenly exclude the other outlets. Islam condemned every form of
prodigal behavior, valorizing military activity instead. At a time
when its neighbors enjoyed a state of equilibrium it commanded
a growing military force that nothing could resist. A renewed critique of the forms of luxury — Protestant at first, then revolutionary — coincided with a possibility of industrial development,
implicit in the technical advances of the new age. The largest share
of the surplus was reserved, in modern times, for capitalist accumulation. Islam rather quickly met its limits; the development
of industry is beginning to approach them in its turn. Islam easily
returned to the forms of equilibrium of the world it had conquered;[12] by contrast, industrial economy is involved in a disorderly agitation: It appears condemned to grow, and already it lacks
the possibility of growing.

The position of Tibet in this schema is in a sense opposite to
those of Islam or the modern world. From time immemorial the
waves of successive invasions from the immense plateaus of central Asia had swept toward the regions where life was easier, to
the east, to the west and to the south. But after the fifteenth century this overflow from the barbarian plateaus ran up against the
effective resistance of cannons.[13] The urban civilization of Tibet
already represented in Central Asia an incipient outlet for the surplus in a different direction. No doubt the hordes of Mongol conquerors used every possibility of invasion (of growth in space)
available to them in their time. Tibet offered itself another solution, which the Mongols themselves were to adopt in turn in the

sixteenth century. The populations of the poor tablelands were periodically condemned to attack the rich areas: *Otherwise they would cease to grow*; they would have to abandon the barbarians' outlet of warfare and find another use for their energy overflow. Monasticism is a mode of expenditure of the excess that Tibet undoubtedly did not discover, but elsewhere it was given a place *alongside* other outlets. In Central Asia the extreme solution consisted in giving the monastery *all* the excess. Today one needs a clear grasp of this principle: A population that cannot somehow develop the system of energy it constitutes, that cannot increase its volume (with the help of new techniques or of wars), must wastefully expend *all* the surplus it is bound to produce. The paradox of Lamaism, which reached a perfect form after the invention of firearms, answered this necessity. It is the radical solution of a country that has no other diversion and ultimately finds itself in a closed container. Not even the outlet consisting in the need to defend oneself, to have resources and human lives available for that purpose. A country that is too poor does not really try. One invades it without occupying it and "the books" that a monk spoke of to Bell could not lie, assuring that Tibet would be invaded from time to time, but no one would stay. Thus, in the midst of a richer and well-armed world, the poor country in its closed container must give the problem of surplus a solution that checks its explosive violence *within*: an internal construction so perfect, so free of controversion, so unconducive to accumulation, that one cannot envisage the least growth of the system. The celibacy of the majority of monks even presented a threat of depopulation. (This was the concern confided to Bell by the commander-in-chief of the army.) The revenue of the monasteries ensured the consumption of resources, supporting a mass of sterile consumers. The equilibrium would soon be jeopardized if this mass were not unproductive and childless. The labor of the laity suffices to feed them, and the resources are such that their number could scarcely be increased. The life of most of the monks is hard (problems would result if there were an advantage in doing nothing). But the parasitism of the lamas resolves the situation so well that the living standard of the Tibetan worker, according to Charles Bell, is higher than that of the Hindu or Chinese worker. Furthermore, writers on Tibet agree in noting the happy disposition of the Tibetans, who sing when they work, are easy to get along with, morally permissive, and light-hearted (yet the winter cold is terrible and the houses have no glass in the windows and no fireplace). The piety of the monks is another matter: It is of secondary importance, but the system would be inconceivable without it. And there is no doubt that lamaic enlightenment morally realizes the essence of consumption, which is to open, to give, to lose, and which brushes calculations aside.

The Tibetan system spread to Mongolia at the end of the sixteenth century. The conversion of the Mongols, even more a change of economy than of religion, was the peculiar dénouement of the history of Central Asia. The age-old outlet of invasions being closed, this last act of the drama defines the meaning of Lamaism: This totalitarian monasticism answers the need to stop the growth of a closed system. Just as Islam reserved all the excess for war, and the modern world for industrial development, Lamaism put everything into the contemplative life, the free play of the sensitive man in the world.

If the different stakes are all played on the same board, then Lamaism is the opposite of the other systems: it alone avoids *activity*, which is always directed toward acquisition and growth. It ceases — true, it has no choice — to subject life to any other ends but life itself: Directly and immediately, life is its own end. In the rites of Tibet the military forms, evoking the age of the kings, are still embodied in the figures of the dances, but as obso-

lete forms whose loss of authority is the object of a ritual representation. In this way the lamas celebrate the victory won over a
world whose violence is crudely unleashed toward the outside.
Their triumph is its unleashing within. But it is no less violent
for all that. In Tibet, even more so than in China, the military
profession is held in contempt. Even after the reforms of the thirteenth Dalai Lama, a family of nobles complained of having had
a son commissioned as an officer. It did no good for Bell to point
out that in England no career was more respected; the parents
begged him to use his influence with the Dalai Lama to support
their request for a cancellation. Of course, while monasticism is a
pure expenditure it is also a renunciation of expenditure; in a sense
it is the perfect solution obtained only by completely turning one's
back to the solution. But one should not underestimate the significance of this bold solution; recent history has accentuated its
paradoxical value. It gives a clear indication concerning the general conditions of economic equilibrium. It confronts human
activity with its limits, and describes – beyond military or productive activity – a world that is unsubordinated by any necessity.

PART FOUR

The Historical Data III

Industrial Society

The Origins of Capitalism

and the Reformation

The Protestant Ethic and the Spirit of Capitalism

Max Weber has shown — not only through analysis but through statistics as well — the privileged role of Protestants in capitalist organization.[1] Even today, in a given region, one sees Protestants being drawn to business and Catholics more to the liberal professions. It seems that there is an affinity between the frame of mind of a hard-working, profit-calculating industrialist and the prosaic severity of the reformed religion. The largest part in this orientation was not played by the doctrines of Luther. But Calvinism's zone of influence (Holland, Great Britain, United States) roughly corresponds to the areas of industrial development. Luther formulated a naive, half-peasant revolt. Calvin expressed the aspirations of the middle class of the commercial cities; his reactions were those of a jurist familiar with business matters.

Weber's arguments, quickly become famous, have been the object of numerous critiques. R.H. Tawney allows that they exaggerated the opposition between Calvinism and the various economic doctrines of its time: It seems that they overlooked the changes that occurred between the initial teaching and the later theory.[2] According to Tawney, up to the second half of the seventeenth century the agreement between the Puritans and capitalism was not complete; moreover, it was less the cause than the effect of the economic givens. But, as Tawney readily acknowledges, these reservations do not necessarily go against Weber's thinking. And on this point he focuses more closely — and somewhat narrowly — on the economic doctrines than on the basic reactions.

In any case Weber deserves the credit for having rigorously analyzed the connection between a religious crisis and the economic turnover that gave rise to the modern world. Others, including Engels, took note of these ties before him, but they did not define their nature.[3] And if there was a later clarification — as in Tawney's work — Weber had emphasized what was essential. The more clearly articulated findings that were obtained subsequently are perhaps of secondary importance.

Economy in the Doctrine and Practice of the Middle Ages

There were contrary types of economy corresponding to two different religious worlds: The ties between the precapitalist economy and Roman Catholicism were just as strong as those between the modern economy and Protestantism. But Weber stressed the fact that the modern economy is essentially capitalist industry, the development of which was not facilitated by the Catholic Church and the state of mind it maintains, whereas in the Protestant world Calvinism provided a favorable starting point. Moreover, it is easier to mark the opposition between the two economic spheres if, going in a direction that takes us farther from Tawney than from Weber, we concentrate first of all on the way the available resources are used. What differentiates the medieval economy from the capitalist economy is that to a very large extent the former, static economy made a nonproductive consumption of the excess wealth, while the latter accumulates and determines a dynamic growth of the production apparatus.

Tawney's is an extensive analysis of Christian economic thought of the Middle Ages. Its basic principle was the subordination of productive activity to the laws of Christian morality. Society, in the thought of the Middle Ages, was a body composed like all living organisms of nonhomogeneous parts, that is, of a hierarchy of functions: The clergy, the military aristocracy and labor formed a unified body in which the component parts of the third term were subservient to the other two (as the trunk and the members are subservient to the head). The producers must satisfy the needs of the nobles and the priests; in exchange, from the former they would receive protection, and from the latter they would receive a share in the divine life and the moral rule to which their activity had to be strictly subordinated. The idea of an economic world independent of the service of the clerics and the nobles, having its autonomy and its own laws as a part of nature, is alien to the thought of the Middle Ages. The seller must part with the merchandise at the *just price*. The just price is defined by the possibility of ensuring the subsistence of the providers. (In a sense, this is the labor value of Marxism, and Tawney sees Marx as "the last of the Scholastics.") Money that is lent cannot be an object of rent, and usury is expressly prohibited by canon law. The scholastics only made allowance cautiously and belatedly for the difference between loans for a business undertaking, which give the creditor a moral right to profit, and those used for the consumption of the borrower, for which no interest is justifiable. The rich man has his reserves: If the poor man becomes destitute, can the rich man who keeps him from dying of hunger, without himself being inconvenienced, demand repayment of more than he advanced? This would be to make time pay; and time, unlike space, was said to be God's domain and not that of men. But time is given in nature: If money always makes it possible somewhere to finance profitable ventures, a natural law gives to the factors "money + time" the additional value of interest (of a share of the possible profit). In this way moral thought is the negation of natural laws; the Church's intervention opposed a free development of the productive forces. Production, according to Christian morality, is a service whose modalities (obligations, responsibilities, prerogatives) are determined by the ends served (by the clerics, in sum, who are the judges of these ends), not by a natural movement. This is a rational and moral — but static — conception of the economic order; it is what a divine, teleological cosmogony is to the idea of evolution determined by a play of forces. The world of the Middle Ages appeared in fact to be given once and for all.

But formal judgments are not the only ones. And the nature of the medieval economy may not be fully disclosed in the writings of the theologians and jurists. It may not be defined in the real practice either, however removed the latter was from the rigor of the theory. A discriminating element may lie in the understanding that a society has of wealth. This understanding is different from the notions commonly expressed by those who had it, and doubtless it would be just as futile to look for it in the opposition of the facts to the theoretical rules. It has to do with the strong and clearly apparent movements that, even unformulated, can determine the nature of an economic system.

Wealth changes meanings according to the advantage we expect from its possession. For John it is the possibility of marriage; for Robert, leisure; for Edward, a change of social standing. But in a given age there are constants. The advantage that matters most, in the capitalist era, is the possibility of investing. This is not a particular point of view: John, Robert and Edward invest their savings with different intentions, and John's intention is the same as Jack's, who is buying a piece of property; but an essential portion of the available resources is set aside for the growth of the produc-

tive forces. It is not the final purpose of any individual in particular, but collectively that of the society that an epoch has chosen.
It gives precedence in the use of the available resources to the
expansion of enterprises and the increase of capital equipment;
in other words, it prefers *an increase of wealth* to its immediate use.

But before the Reformation this was not yet the case. The possibility of an increase was not given. A development is induced
by an opening-up of unexploited territories, by technical changes,
or by the appearance of new products from which new needs arise.
But a society can also be led to consume all its products. Hence
it must somehow destroy the surplus resources it has at its disposal. Idleness is the simplest means for this purpose. The man
of leisure destroys the products necessary for his subsistence no
less fully than does fire. But the worker who labors at the construction of a pyramid destroys those products just as uselessly:
From the standpoint of profit the pyramid is a monumental mistake; one might just as well dig an enormous hole, then refill it
and pack the ground. We obtain the same result if we ingest a
substance, such as alcohol, whose consumption does not enable
us to work more – or even deprives us, for a time, of our strength
to produce. Idleness, the pyramid or alcohol have the advantage
of consuming without a return – without a profit – the resources
that they use: They simply *satisfy* us; they correspond to the *unnec-
essary choice* that we make of them. In a society whose productive forces do not increase – or increase little – this satisfaction,
in its collective form, determines the value of wealth, and thus
the nature of the economy. The moral principles and rules by
which production is closely bound (but at times in completely
superficial ways) mean less than this satisfaction that decides the
use of products (at least the use of what remains available beyond
subsistence). It was not the theories of the Schoolmen that defined
the economic society, but rather the need it had for the satisfac-

tion of cathedrals and abbeys, idle priests and monks. In other words, the possibility of good *deeds satisfying to God* (satisfaction in medieval society could not nominally be that of man) generally determined the mode of consumption of the available resources.

This religious determination of the economy is not surprising; it even defines religion. Religion is the satisfaction that a society gives to the use of excess resources, or rather to their destruction (at least insofar as they are useful). This is what gives religions their rich material aspect, which only ceases to be *conspicuous* when an emaciated spiritual life withdraws from labor a time that could have been employed in producing. The only point is the absence of utility, the *gratuitousness* of these collective determinations. They do render a *service*, true, in that men attribute to these gratuitous activities consequences in the realm of supernatural efficacy; but they are useful on that plane precisely insofar as they are gratuitous, insofar as they are needless consumptions of resources first and foremost.

Religious activities — sacrifices, festivals, luxurious amenities — absorb the excess energy of a society, but a secondary efficacy is usually attributed to a thing whose primary meaning was in breaking the chain of efficacious actions. This results in a great malaise — a feeling of wrong, of dupery — which pervades the religious sphere. A sacrifice in view of a crude result, such as fertility of the fields, is experienced as a commonplace action at the level of the *divine*, of the *sacred*, which religion calls into play. In theory, *salvation* in Christianity liberates the ends of religious life from the domain of productive activity. But if the faithful's salvation is the reward for his merits, if he can achieve it by his deeds, then he has simply brought more closely into the domain of religion the concatenation that makes useful work wretched in his eyes. Hence those *deeds* by which a Christian tries to win his salvation can in turn be considered profanations. Even the mere fact of choosing salvation as a goal appears contrary to the truth of grace. Grace alone brings about an accord with the divinity, which cannot be subjected to casual series as *things* can. The gift that divinity makes of itself to the faithful soul cannot be paid for.

The Moral Position of Luther

The medieval practice of charity, the religious communities and the mendicant monks, the festivities and the pilgrimages perhaps did not incense Luther so much because of their abuses: What Luther rejected was mainly the idea of merits acquired by these means.[4] He condemned an extravagant economic regime for its contradiction with the Gospel's principle of hostility to wealth and luxury; but he did not so much object to luxury itself as to the possibility of gaining heaven by making an extravagant use of individual wealth. He seemed to concentrate his thinking on a point where a divine world appeared free from compromise and completely unconnected with the machinations of this world. Through the buying of indulgences, the faithful Roman Catholic could even employ his resources to purchase a time in paradise (in fact these resources contributed to clerical opulence and idleness). The Lutheran conception was radically opposed to this; it provided no means (other than sin) of removing wealth from utility and rendering it to the world of glory. The disciple of Luther could not *accomplish* anything here below that was not futile – or culpable – whereas the follower of Rome was urged to make the Church the earthly radiance of God. But in making divinity radiate in the works of this world, Rome was reducing it to base actions. The only recourse, in the eyes of a Luther, appeared to lie in a decisive separation between God and everything that was not the deep inner life of faith, everything that we can *do* and *really* carry into effect.

Wealth was thus deprived of meaning, apart from its productive value. Contemplative idleness, giving to the poor and the splendor of ceremonies and churches ceased to have the least worth or were considered a sign of the devil. Luther's doctrine is the utter negation of a system of intense consumption of resources. An immense army of secular and regular clergy squandered the surplus riches of Europe, inciting the nobles and the merchants to rival squanderings. This was the scandal that provoked Luther, but he was only able to oppose it with a more complete negation of the world. In making a gigantic waste the means of opening the gates of heaven to mankind, the Church gave a painful impression: It had succeeded less in making earth heavenly than in making heaven banal. At the same time it had turned its back on all its possibilities. But it had kept the economy relatively stable. It is a singular fact that the Roman Church, in the image that a medieval village has left of the world it created, represented in a felicitous way the effect of an immediate use of wealth. This came about in a tangle of contradictions, but the light it cast has found its way to us: Shining through the world of pure utility that succeeded it, where wealth lost its immediate value, it still radiates in our eyes.

Calvinism

Luther's reaction remained strictly negative. In his view, however powerless man was to please God in his earthly activity, the latter must still be subject to moral law. Luther upheld the Church's traditional curse against usury and generally had the aversion for business that was inherent in the archaic conception of the economy. But Calvin abandoned the doctrinal condemnation of loans at interest and generally recognized the morality of commerce. "What reason is there why the income from business should not be larger than that from landowning? Whence do the merchant's profits come except from his own diligence and industry?"[5] For this reason Weber gives Calvinism a decisive role in the formation of the capitalist spirit. From the first it was the religion of the commercial bourgeoisie of Geneva and the Netherlands. Calvin had a sense of the conditions and importance of economic development; he spoke as a jurist and a practical man. Tawney, following Weber, underscores the significance of his thought for the bourgeois world to which it gave expression. According to Tawney, he was to the bourgeoisie of his time what Marx was to the proletariat of ours: He provided the organization and the doctrine.[6]

On a basic level, the doctrine has the same meaning as that of Luther. Calvin rejects merit and works no less firmly than Luther does, but his principles, articulated a little differently, also have more consequences. In Tawney's view the aim is not "personal salvation, but the glorification of God, to be sought, not by prayer only, but by action – the sanctification of the world by strife and labor. For Calvinism, with all its repudiation of personal merit, is intensely practical. Good works are not a way of attaining salvation, but they are indispensable as a proof that salvation has been attained."[7] Deprived of the value that the Church had given them, works are reintroduced in a sense, but they are different works. The negation of practices involving a needless expenditure of wealth is no less complete than in the doctrine of Luther, in that value was withdrawn from contemplative idleness, from ostentatious luxury and from the forms of charity that maintained nonproductive poverty, and given to the virtues that have their basis in utility: The reformed Christian had to be humble, saving, hardworking (he had to bring the greatest zeal to his profession, be it in commerce, industry or whatever); he even had to help eliminate begging, which went against principles whose norm was productive activity.[8]

Calvinism in a sense carried the overturning of values effected by Luther to its extreme consequence. Calvin did not just repudiate those forms of divine beauty to which the Church laid claim. Limiting man's possibility to useful works, what he offered man as a means of glorifying God was the negation of his own glory. The true sanctity of Calvinist works resided in the abandonment of sanctity — in the renunciation of any life that might have in this world a halo of splendor. The sanctification of God was thus linked to the desacralization of human life. This was a wise solution because once the futility of good works was established, there remained a man with the power, or rather the necessity, of acting, to whom it was not enough to say that deeds are unavailing. Attachment to a profession, to the task that the social complex assigns the individual, was nothing very new, but until then it had not taken on the deep significance and conclusive value that Calvinism gave it. The decisions to rescue divine glory from the compromises in which the Church had placed it could not have had a more radical consequence than the relegation of mankind to gloryless activity.

The Distant Effect of the Reformation:
The Autonomy of the World of Production

If, following Weber, one considers this position as it relates to the spirit of capitalism, one cannot imagine anything more favorable to the rise of industry. A condemnation of idleness and luxury on the one hand, an affirmation of the value of enterprise on the other. Immediate use of the infinite wealth that is the universe being strictly reserved for God, man for his part was unreservedly dedicated to labor, to the allocation of wealth — time, materiel and every kind of resource — to the development of the production apparatus.

Tawney points out nonetheless that capitalism requires an additional element: It is an unrestricted growth of impersonal productive forces; it is the liberation of the natural movement of the economy, whose general momentum depends on the individual pursuit of profit. Capitalism is not just an accumulation of riches for commercial, financial or industrial ventures, but general individualism, free enterprise. Capitalism could not have coexisted with the old economic legislation, whose moral principle was the subordination of enterprise to society, which imposed price controls, combatted financial schemes and placed serious restrictions on loans at interest. Tawney observes that in the countries where Calvinism was dominant (this was the case in Geneva, with Calvin and Theodorus Beza, or in Scotland, with John Knox), it tended toward a collective dictatorship.[9] But it was only "a minority, living on the defensive beneath the suspicious eyes of a hostile government"; it slipped toward extreme individualism. In reality it was only in England, in the second half of the seventeenth century, that Puritans linked the principle of the free pursuit of profit to the Calvinist tradition. It was only at that late date that the independence of economic laws was posited, and that the abdication of the moral sovereignty of the religious world in the sphere of production came to pass. But the lateness of this development is a fact whose importance should not be exaggerated. Implicit in the first formulation, it needed to resolve a basic difficulty. What was crucially at stake in the Reformation, from the economic standpoint, did not so much depend on the stating of principles as on the swaying of minds; the latter could not effectively be achieved except on one condition, that it be concealed at first. The change would be meaningful only if it was the doing of men of unassailable moral authority, speaking to down-to-earth interests on behalf of higher powers. What was needed was less to give complete freedom to the natural impulses of the merchants than to tie them to some dominant moral position. It was first a matter of destroying the authority that founded the medieval economy. This could not have been done by stating the principle of capitalist interest directly. What accounts for the late moment when the consequences of the doctrines of the Reformation emerged is the difficulty of defending the nature of capitalism *a priori*. It is remarkable that the spirit and the ethic of capitalism have almost never been expressed in a pure form. It is only by way of an exception that one can say, as Weber does concerning those principles, set forth in the middle of the eighteenth century by Benjamin Franklin, that they express the spirit of capitalism with an almost classical purity. But in citing them, I will show in fact that it would have been impossible to give them free rein without a preamble — without first giving them the mask of an inaccessible divinity.

Franklin writes:

Remember that time is money. He that can earn ten shillings a day by his labour, and goes abroad, or sits idle, one half of that day, though he spends but sixpence during his diversion or idleness, ought not to reckon *that* the only expense; he has really spent, or rather thrown away, five shillings besides. Remember, that money is of the prolific, generating nature. Money can beget money, and its offspring can beget more, and so on. Five shillings turned is six, turned again it is seven and threepence, and so on, till it becomes a hundred pounds. The more there is of it, the more it produces every turning, so that the profits rise quicker and quicker. He that kills a breeding-sow, destroys all her offspring to the thousandth generation. He that murders a crown, destroys all that it might have produced, even scores of pounds.

Nothing is more cynically opposed to the spirit of religious sacrifice, which continued, prior to the Reformation, to justify an immense unproductive consumption and the idleness of all those who had a free choice in life. Of course, Franklin's principle — seldom formulated — continues to guide the economy (toward an impasse no doubt). But in Luther's time it could not be stated in overt opposition to that of the Church.

If one now considers the spiritual movement whose slow progress through the doctrinal meanders goes from Luther's scandalized trip to Rome to Franklin's laborious candor, a privileged direction emerges. But the impression is not that of a resolute and determined movement, and if there is a constancy in the direction, it appears to be given from the outside, in the demands of the productive forces. The mind tries gropingly to answer these demands — in fact its hesitation helps it to do so — but only the objective demands move things hesitantly toward the goal. This is somewhat contrary to the thinking of Max Weber, who is credited, perhaps wrongly, with having assigned an intrinsic shaping power to religion. But it is certain that the revolution effected by the Reformation has, as Weber saw, a profound significance: It marked the passage to a new form of economy. Referring back to the spirit of the great reformers, one can even say that by accepting the extreme consequences of a demand for religious purity it destroyed the sacred world, the world of nonproductive consumption, and handed the earth over to the men of production, to the bourgeois. This does not alter the primary meaning of those consequences: In the sphere of religion they were extreme (and already impossible as such). However, in the economic order they only represented a beginning; yet it cannot be denied that they inaugurated the world of the bourgeoisie, whose accomplishment is economic mankind.

The Bourgeois World

The Fundamental Contradiction of the Search for Intimacy in Works

At the origin of industrial society, based on the primacy and autonomy of commodities, of *things*, we find a contrary impulse to place what is essential — *what causes one to tremble with fear and delight* — outside the world of activity, the world of *things*. But however this is shown it does not controvert the fact that in general a capitalist society reduces what is human to the condition of a *thing* (of a commodity). Religion and economy were delivered in one and the same movement from that which indebted them to one another: the former from profane calculation, the latter from limits given from the outside. But this fundamental opposition (this unexpected contradiction) is more interesting than it might seem at first. The problem that Calvinism so boldly solved is not limited to the interest that the historical study of religious matters always arouses. In fact it is still the problem that dominates us. Religion in general answered the desire that man always had to find himself, to regain an intimacy that was always strangely lost. But the mistake of all religion is to always give man a contradictory answer: *an external form of intimacy*. So the successive solutions only exacerbate the problem: Intimacy is never separated from external elements, without which it could not be *signified*. Where we think we have caught hold of the Grail, we have only grasped a *thing*, and what is left in our hands is only a cooking pot....

Man's current quest does not differ from those of Galahad or Calvin either in its object or in the disappointment that comes once the object is found. But the modern world goes about it in a different way: It does not look for anything illusory and it means to achieve an essential conquest by directly solving the problems that are posed by *things*. Perhaps it is absolutely right: Often a complete separation seems necessary. If we are in search of an object of possession, then we can only propose to look for *things*, since only *things* are within the province of activity and the search always commits us to activity. The Protestant critique of the Roman Church (i.e., of the pursuit of activity expressed in works) was not due to a strange scruple; and its ultimate (indirect) consequence, which commits mankind only to *do* — without any further aim — that which can be done *in the order of things*, is indeed the only solution. But if man is to find himself in the end, he looks in vain when he follows the paths that have led him to self-estrangement. All he could expect by following them was to adapt, for service, those *things* that are such, however, only to serve him.

It is reasonable then to think that man cannot rediscover his truth without solving the problem of economy; but with respect to this *necessary* condition, he can say and believe it is *sufficient*, he can affirm that he will be free once he has complied with the exigencies given in *things* that are necessary, in the physical arrangements without which his needs cannot be satisfied.

An obstacle will stop him, however: He will not be able to grasp that which he is bereft of any better than if he had taken paths more open to criticism; what he grasps will be no different from what was grasped by those who preceded him in his quest: As always he will only catch hold of *things* and will take the shadow which they are for the prey he was hunting.

I maintain that the argument according to which the solution of the material problem is *sufficient* is the most admissible one at first.[10] But even if the solution of the problems of life — the key to which is a man's not becoming merely *a thing*, but of *being in a sovereign manner* — were the unavoidable consequence of a satisfactory response to material exigencies, it remains radically distinct from that response, with which it is often confused.

For this reason I can say concerning Calvinism, having capitalism as a consequence, that it poses a fundamental problem: *How can man find himself — or regain himself — seeing that the action to which the search commits him in one way or another is precisely what estranges him from himself?*

The different statements, in modern times, of this disconcerting problem help to make us aware both of what is at issue now, in history, and of the projected fulfillment that is offered us.

The Resemblance Between the Reformation and Marxism

Considering the course followed by the reformers and its consequences, would it be paradoxical to conclude: "It put an end to the relative stability and equilibrium of a world in which man was less estranged from himself than we are at present"? It would be easy in fact to find ourselves personally looking for a form of humanity that does not betray it, shunning those vacant lots, those suburbs and factories, whose appearance expresses the nature of industrial societies, and making our way toward some dead city, bristling with gothic spires. We cannot deny that present-day humanity has lost the secret, kept until the current age, of giving itself a face in which it might recognize the splendor that is proper to it. Doubtless the "works" of the Middle Ages in a sense were only *things*: They could rightly appear worthless to anyone who envisioned, beyond, in its inaccessible purity, the wealth that he attributed to God. And yet the medieval representation of society has the power today of evoking that "lost intimacy."[11]

A church is perhaps a *thing*: It is little different from a barn, which clearly is a thing. A *thing* is what we know from without, what is given to us as a physical reality (verging on a utility, available without reserve). We cannot penetrate a *thing*, and it has no meaning other than its material qualities, adapted or not to some useful purpose, in the productive sense of the word. But the church expresses an intimate feeling and addresses itself to intimate feeling. It is perhaps the *thing* that a building is, but the *thing* that a barn really is is adapted to the gathering in of the crops: It comes down to the physical qualities that were given to it, measuring the costs against the anticipated advantages, in order to subordinate it to that use. The expression of intimacy in the church corresponds rather to the needless consumption of labor: From the start the purpose of the edifice withdraws it from public utility, and this first movement is accentuated in a profusion of useless ornaments. For the construction of a church is not a profitable use of the available labor, but rather its consumption, the destruction of its utility. Intimacy is not expressed by a *thing* except on one condition: that this *thing* be essentially the opposite of a *thing*, the opposite of a product, of a commodity[12] – a consumption and a sacrifice. Since intimate feeling is a consumption, it is consumption that expresses it, not a *thing*, which is its negation. The capitalist bourgeoisie relegated the construction of churches to a subordinate plane, preferring to construct factories instead. But the Church dominated the whole system of the Middle Ages. It erected its steeples wherever men were grouped together for common works: Thus it was clear and visible from afar that the basest works had a higher purpose, apart from their tangible interest;

this purpose was the glory of God, but is not God in a sense a *distant* expression of man, in the anguish of the depths he perceives?

That said, the longing for a bygone world is nonetheless based on a limited judgment. The regret that I might have for a time when the obscure intimacy of the animal was scarcely distinguished from the immense flux of the world indicates a power that is truly lost, but it fails to recognize what matters more to me. Even if he has lost the world in leaving animality behind, man has nonetheless become that *consciousness* of having lost it which we are, and which is more, in a sense, than a possession of which the animal is not conscious: It is *man*, in a word, being that which alone matters to me and which the animal cannot be. Likewise the romantic longing for the Middle Ages is in fact only an abandonment. It has the meaning of a protest against the rise of industry, versus the nonproductive use of resources; it correlates with the opposition to the values given in the cathedrals of capitalist interest (to which modern society can be reduced). This longing refuses to see, at the basis of the industrial rise, the spirit of contestation and change, the need to go from all parts to the limit of the world's possibilities. It can doubtless be said of the Protestant critique of *saintly works* that it gave the world over to profane works, that the demand for divine purity only managed to exile the divine, and to complete man's separation from it. It can be said, finally, that starting then *things* dominated man, insofar as he lived for enterprise and less and less in the present time. But domination is never total, and in a deep sense it is only a comedy: It never deceives more than partly, while in the propitious darkness a new truth turns stormy.

The Protestant positing of an unattainable divinity, irreducible to the action-bound mind, no longer has any real meaning for us. One could even declare it absent from the world (having lost its connection to that uncompromising demand, the current

Protestant way of thinking is more *human*), as if the positing were itself bound to resemble the divinity it defined. But this absence may be illusory, analogous to that of the traitor whom no one denounces and who is everywhere. In a limited sense, the Reformation has ceased to exert any action; yet it survives in the rigors of consciousness, in the lack of naiveté, in the maturity of the modern world. Given the lethargy of the multitude, Calvin's subtle demand for integrity, the sharp-edged tension of reason (which is not satisfied with little and is never satisfied with itself) and an *extremist* and *rebellious* way of thinking take on the appearance of a pathetic vigil. The multitude has surrendered to the somnolence of production, living the mechanical existence — half-ludicrous, half-revolting – of *things*. But conscious thought reaches the last degree of alertness in the same movement. On the one hand it pursues, in an extension of technical activity, the investigation that leads to an increasingly clear and distinct knowledge of *things*. In itself science limits consciousness to objects; it does not lead to *self-consciousness* (it can know the subject only by taking it for an object, for a *thing*); but it contributes to the wakefulness by accustoming us to precision and by *disappointing* us: For it acknowledges its limits, it admits its powerlessness to arrive at *self-consciousness*. On the other hand, thought does not at all abandon, in the face of industrial development, man's basic desire to find himself (to have a sovereign existence) beyond a useful action that he cannot avoid. This desire has only become more insistent. Protestantism referred man's encounter with his truth to the other world. Marxism, which inherited its rigor, and gave a precise form to disorderly impulses, denies even more than Calvinism a tendency of man to look for himself directly when he acts; it resolutely excludes the foolishness of sentimental action.[13] By reserving action for the changing of the material organization, Marx clearly formulated that which Calvin had merely outlined, a radical independence of *things* (of the economy) in relation to other (religious or, generally, affective) concerns. Conversely, he implied the independence, with respect to action, of the return movement of man to himself (to the profundity, the intimacy of his being). This movement can take place only after the liberation is achieved, and only after the action is completed.

This specific aspect of Marxism is usually overlooked: Marxism is charged with the confusion of which I speak above. For Marx, "the solution of the material problem is *sufficient*," but for man the fact "of not *being* merely *like a thing*, but of *being in a sovereign manner*," in theory given as "its unavoidable consequence," nonetheless remains different from "a satisfactory response to material demands." Marx's originality in this regard lies in his wanting to achieve a moral result only negatively, by the elimination of material obstacles. This leads people to attribute an exclusive concern with material goods to him; they fail to notice, in the provocative clarity, his utter discretion and his aversion for religious forms whereby man's truth is subordinated to hidden ends. The fundamental proposition of Marxism is to free the world of *things* (of the economy) entirely from every element that is extraneous to *things* (to the economy): It was by going to the limit of the possibilities implied in *things* (by complying with their demands without reservation, by replacing the government of particular interests with the "government of things," by carrying to its ultimate consequences the movement that reduces man to the condition of a *thing*, that Marx was determined to reduce *things* to the condition of man, and man to the free disposition of himself.

In this perspective of man liberated through action, having effected a perfect adequation of himself to *things*, man would have them behind him, as it were; they would no longer enslave him. A new chapter would begin, where man would finally be free to return to his own intimate truth, to freely dispose of the being that he *will be*, that he is not now because he is servile.

But by the very fact of this position (which, as far as intimacy is concerned, dissolves away, offers nothing), Marxism is less the completion of the Calvinist project than a critique of capitalism, which it reproaches with having liberated *things* without rigor, without any other end, without any other law than chance — and private interest.

The World of Modern Industry, or, The Bourgeois World

Capitalism in a sense is an unreserved surrender to *things*, heedless of consequences and seeing nothing beyond them. For common capitalism, *things* (products and production) are not, as for the Puritans, what is becoming and wants to become; if things are within it, if it is itself the *thing*, this is in the way that Satan inhabits the soul of someone possessed, unbeknown to him, or that the possessed, without knowing it, is Satan himself.

Self-denial, which in Calvinism was the affirmation of God, was an unattainable ideal in a sense: It could be the act of strong personalities, capable of imposing the values with which they identified, but exceptions always came into play. On the other hand, freedom given to things was the common possibility. There was no need to maintain the purest — and poorest — spirituality, which alone was rigorous enough in the beginning to counterbalance the subjection of the whole body and of activity to *things*. But once the principle of servitude was granted, the world of *things* (the world of modern industry) could develop of itself, without any further thought of the absent God. The advantage was clear, in minds always quick to grasp the *real* object, of allowing intimacy to recede beyond the threshold of consciousness. The reign of things was supported, moreover, by the natural propensity to servitude. It corresponded in the same movement to that *pure* will to power (to growth for its own sake) that, outwardly contrary to the servile spirit, is basically only its complement. In the service of a power that is not used — the perfect form of the absorption of resources in growth — is found the only genuine nullification, the least slippery renunciation of life. But this attitude is often difficult to distinguish from that of the pure Calvinist, although it is the latter's opposite.

At least the Calvinist was at the highest point of alertness and tension. The man of industrial growth — having no other purpose than growth — on the contrary is the expression of somnolence. No tension around him, no desire to adapt a world to his standards. The men whose action resulted in modern industry were not even aware, the idea not having occurred to them, that such a world might be possible: They were utterly unconcerned about an impotence in the movement that carried them along, that could not reduce the world to its law. They even used, for the development of enterprise, the openings that were maintained by the continued existence of various movements contrary to theirs. In the capitalist world there was no principled preference given to the production of the means of production (this preference was to appear only in communist accumulation). The bourgeoisie was unaware of any opposition between the primacy of growth and its contraries: unproductive expenditures of all sorts, institutions and values that create expenditures. The opposition only concerned (and only affected) the amount of the expenditure. Bourgeois capitalism was opposed to luxury, but only in a feeble and illogical way: Its avarice and its action did actually reduce luxury, but if one excludes the uncalculated effects, it never departed from laissez-faire.

Thus the bourgeoisie created the world of confusion. It was essentially a world of *things*, but as man's reduction was no longer linked to his nullification before God, all that did not enter into the sleep of growth suffered from the abandonment of the search for a beyond. However, no paths were closed: Precisely because *things* generally prevailed and dominated the movement of the multitude, all the aborted dreams remained available; life (the global movement of life) became detached from them no doubt, but they still serve as consolation for troubled beings. A chaos began, where, in the most contrary ways, everything became equally possible. Society's unity was maintained owing to the unquestioned importance and success of the dominant activity. In this uncertainty, the temptations of the past easily survived their invalidation. The contradictions to which they had led ceased to be felt, in a world where reality was all the more hateful for being publicly the measure of man. The romantic protest itself was free. But that freedom in every sense meant that man, regarded in his unity (in the undifferentiated aggregate), consented to be only a *thing*.

The Resolution of Material Difficulties and the Radicalism of Marx

To the extent that mankind is in complicity with the bourgeoisie (on the *whole*, that is), it vaguely consents to be nothing more (as mankind) than *things*. Yet it is within this confused multitude, and tied to confusion as a plant is tied to the ground, that the spirit of rigor proliferates. Its essence is in wanting – through a completion of *things*, an adequation of *things* (of production) and man – the access or return of man to himself. And to the extent that this rigor has the goal of developing the pure sciences and the techniques, the bourgeois world leaves it an open field.

Within the limits of strictly economic activity, the rigor has a precise object: the dedication of excess resources to the removal of life's difficulties and to the reduction of labor time. This is the only use of wealth that coincides with an adequation of man to *things* and it retains the negative character of action, whose goal for man remains the possibility of being entirely at his own disposal. The spirit of rigor, tied to the development of the sciences and techniques, is well equipped for this fundamental operation. But the use of the comfort and the myriad services of industrial civilization cannot be limited to a small number of privileged persons: Sumptuary use had functions; it manifested values and it implied the connection between wealth and the responsibility of manifesting those values. But this manifestation resulted from the error that makes us want to grasp, like things, that which is predicated on the negation of things. The spirit of rigor is thus committed to destroying the remnants of the ancient world. The capitalist law leaves it free to develop the material possibilities that it bears within it, but at the same time tolerates privileges that hinder this development. Under these conditions, the rigor quickly leads one to draw from the sciences and techniques the consequences that reduce the chaos of the present world to the rigor of *things* themselves, which is the rational linking together of all the operations on *things*. It then has a revolutionary significance that Marx formulated in a sovereign way.

The Remnants of Feudalism and Religion

The necessity of first eliminating the values of the past must be made clear, however. In the economic system of the Middle Ages wealth was unevenly distributed between those who manifested the accepted values, in the name of which wealth was wasted, and those who furnished the wasted labor.[14] The work of the fields or the towns thus had a servile quality with respect to the values manifested, but so did the worker with respect to the clerics and nobles. These latter *claimed* not to be *things*, but the quality of *thinghood*, verbal protests notwithstanding, fell squarely on the worker. This original situation has a specific consequence: One cannot expect to liberate man by going to the limit of the possibilities of *things* and nonetheless leave free, as capitalism does, those who have no other reason for being than the negation of work, which is base, in favor of more elevated activities, asserted to be the only ones capable of restoring man to himself. In a sense, the remnants of feudalism and religion, which capitalism overlooks, represent the immutable and unconscious desire to make a *thing* of the worker. Comparatively, the worker can only be a *thing* if we liberate ourselves by devoting ourselves to an activity that repudiates the labor of the worker. The fulfillment of things (the complete adequation of man to production) can have a liberating effect only if the old values, tied to nonproductive expenditures, are denounced and dismantled, as the Roman values were during the Reformation. Indeed, there is no doubt that man's return to himself implies first of all that the deceitful faces of the aristocracy and of religion be unmasked, for they are not really the face of man, but his appearance lent to things. Man's return to himself cannot be confused with the error of those who claim to grasp intimacy as one grasps a loaf of bread or a hammer.

Communism and Man's Adequation to the Utility of Things

A radical position, to which the working-class world has given its political consequences, emerges from the above. In a sense it is a strange position. It is first of all a radical affirmation of real material forces, and a no less radical negation of spiritual values. The communists always give precedence to *things*, as against that which dares not have their subordinate character. This attitude is based solidly on the tastes of the proletarians, who commonly lack a sense of spiritual values, who of their own accord reduce man's interest to interest pure and simple, and who see the human universe as a system of *things* subordinated to one another: the plow ploughs the field, the field produces wheat, the wheat feeds the blacksmith, who forges the plow. This in no way excludes the higher aspirations, but these are changeable, vague, open, by contrast with those of the old type of populations, which are usually traditional and immutable. Indeed, the proletarians undertake man's liberation starting from *things* (to which they were reduced by a world whose values were almost inaccessible to them). They do not involve him in ambitious projects; they do not construct a rich and variegated world, modeled on the ancient mythologies or the medieval theologies. Their attention is apt to be limited to *what is there*, but they are not closely bound by the elevated phrases that express their feelings. In their universe there is no firm limit opposed to the general linkage of *things subordinating one another*. A rigorously practical politics, a brutal politics, reducing its reasons to strict reality, is still what best corresponds to their passion, a politics that reveals the intentions of a selfish group, and is all the more ruthless. A militant of this persuasion is easily reduced to a strict subordination. He readily accepts being finally reduced, by the work of liberation, to the condition of a *thing*, which is the case, for example, when discipline prescribes two contradictory slogans in succession. This radical attitude has a strange consequence: It gives to the bourgeois, to the exploitation which the workers want to abolish, the feeling of upholding freedom for mankind, of avoiding the reduction of individuals to *things*. And yet, what is involved is only an enormous effort whose aim is self-determination.

In actual fact, the bourgeois cannot really forget that the freedom of their world is the freedom of confusion. In the end they are merely helpless. The immense results of working-class politics, the generalized provisional servitude that is its only sure consequence, frightens them, but they can only bemoan the situation. They no longer have a sense of their historical mission; the fact is that as a response to the ascendant movement of the communists, they cannot give rise to the least hope.

PART FIVE

The Present Data

Soviet Industrialization

The Distress of Noncommunist Humanity

It has always been possible to say, "The moral emptiness of today's world is appalling." To some degree the fact of never being assured defines the future, just as that of having an impenetrable night ahead of one defines the present. Yet there are good reasons at present for dwelling on the distress. I am thinking not so much of the increased danger of catastrophe – more invigorating than it appears – as of the absence of faith, or rather the absence of ideas, that abandons modern thought to impotence. Thirty years ago a number of conflicting speculations illuminated a future that was adapted to man. The general belief in indefinite progress made the entire planet and all time to come a domain that seemed at one's disposal without restriction. Since then the situation has greatly changed. When a crushing victory ensured the return to peace, a feeling of *inferiority* vis-à-vis the inevitable problems gradually seized hold of the majority. Only the communist world –the USSR and affiliated parties – was an exception, a monolith in the midst of an anguished, incoherent humanity, possessing no other unity than anguish.

Far from helping to maintain a fragile optimism, this bloc – which possesses an unshakeable assurance on its own behalf – is making the distress complete. A boundless hope for itself, it is at the same time a terror for those who reject its law and do not automatically concur with its principles. Marx and Engels exclaimed in 1847 (these are the first words of the *Manifesto*): "A specter is haunting Europe – the specter of Communism." In 1949 communism ceased to be a phantom: It is a state and an army (by far the most powerful *on earth*), supplemented by an organized movement and maintained in a monolithic cohesion by a negation of every form of personal interest. And Europe is not alone in being shaken, but Asia as well; despite its military and industrial superiority, America itself is growing tense, and the indignation it expresses in the name of narrow individualism poorly conceals an exasperated fear. Today the fear of the USSR obsesses and disheartens the whole noncommunist world. Nothing is resolved, sure of itself, endowed with an uncompromising will to organize, except for the USSR. Essentially, the rest of the world lines up against the latter through inertia: It willingly surrenders to the contradictions that it bears within it; it lives from day to day, blind, rich or poor, *depressed*, and its speech has become an impotent protest – even a groan.

The Intellectual Positions with Regard to Communism

In the absence of ascendant ideas, in the absence of a hope that would unite and elevate, human thought in Western Europe and America is now situated first and foremost in relation to the doctrine and the reality of the Soviet Union. That doctrine has many proponents who make the dictatorship of the proletariat and the abolition of capitalism the preliminary conditions of a satisfied human life. The basic aim of the Soviet state is, according to the Constitution of 1918, "suppressing all exploitation of man by man, abolishing forever the division of society into classes, ruthlessly suppressing all exploiters, bringing about the socialist organization of society and the triumph of socialism in all countries." The goal of first achieving "socialism in one country," and the paths that the Russian revolution has followed since 1918 have provoked the opposition of certain communist elements. But thus far only the faithful supporters of the Soviet Union, determined to remain in harmony with it and carry out the revolution in their country, have been able to derive from their opinion the force to unite the working masses. The communist dissidence has shared the sterility of the other active tendencies within the democracies. For it is informed by an aversion, a rejection, and not by a resolute hope arising from its own resolution.

Moreover, the reaction of the opponents has two contrary sources. In the first place, the ramifications of the principles of the Soviet Union have been limited by the given conditions: The domain of socialism has been limited not just to a single country, but to an underdeveloped industrial country. According to Marx, socialism would result from an extreme development of productive forces: Present-day American society, and not the Russian society of 1917, would be ripe for socialism. Furthermore, Lenin saw in the October revolution the beginning movement — diverted — of a world revolution. Later, Stalin, in opposition to Trotsky, ceased to make world revolution a precondition for the building of socialism in Russia. In any case the Soviet Union came to accept the game it had meant to avoid. But apparently, contrary to Trotsky's optimism, there was no choice in the matter.

The consequences of "socialism in one country" cannot be disregarded. To say nothing of material difficulties, without any connection to those a global socialism would encounter, the fact of being bound to one nation could alter the revolution, giving it a composite form difficult to decipher and deceiving in appearance.

But here it is the reactionary aspect of "Stalinism" that provokes the opposition. From another angle, the criticism of the "anti-Stalinists" ties in with that of anticommunism in general.

A resolute contempt for individual interest, for thought, for personal conventions and rights has characterized the Bolshevik revolution from the start. In this regard, Stalin's policy brings out the traits of Lenin's, but does not break new ground. "Bolshevik firmness" opposes "corrupt liberalism." Hatred of communism, so general and so strong nowadays, has its primary source in that complete negation, pushed to its extreme consequences, of individual reality. For the noncommunist world in general, the individual is the ultimate end; value and truth are referred to the solitude of a private life, deaf and blind to that which it is not (they are referred, more precisely, to its economic independence). At the basis of the democratic idea (the bourgeois idea) of the individual, there is assuredly deception, avarice and a negation of man as an element of destiny (of the universal action of that which is); the modern bourgeois appears as the poorest figure of a person that humanity has assumed, but to this "person" inured to the isolation — and mediocrity — of his life, communism offers a death leap. To be sure, the "person" refuses to leap, but does not become a stirring hope for that fact. The revolutionaries who concur in his anguish are embarrassed by it. But Stalinism is so radical that its communist opponents have ended up in concert with the bourgeois. This collusion, whether conscious or not, has greatly contributed to the weakness and inertia of all those who wanted to escape the rigor of Stalinist communism.

Beyond simple feelings such as adherence, opposition or hatred, the complexity of Stalinism, the indecipherable figure that the conditions of its development have given it, is apt to provoke the most confused *intellectual* reactions. Without a doubt, one of the most serious problems for the Soviet Union today is tied to the national form that socialism has taken there. For a long time a parallel was drawn between certain external features of Hitlerite socialism, so-called, and those of Stalinist socialism: a leader, a single party, importance of the army, a youth organization, negation of individual thought, and repression. The aims and the socioeconomic structures were radically different, setting the two systems in mortal opposition to each other, but the similarity of methods was striking. The emphasis that was placed on the form and even on the national traditions focused attention on these dubious comparisons. Moreover, this kind of criticism linked the opposition communists to bourgeois liberalism: A movement of "antitotalitarian" opinion has formed which tends to paralyze action; its strictly conservative effect is certain.

Thought is so deeply disturbed by this paradoxical situation that it is given over, sporadically, to the most hazardous interpretations. They are not always printed. I will mention the following one, which is brilliant if not solid. It seems that Stalinism is not at all the analogue of Hitlerism; on the contrary, it is not a *national* but rather an *imperial socialism*. Moreover, *imperial* is to be understood in a sense opposite to that of the imperialism of a nation: The word would refer to the necessity of an *empire*, that is, of a *universal state* that would put an end to the economic and military anarchy of the present age. *National Socialism* was bound to fail, for its very principles limited its scope to one nation: There was no way to incorporate the conquered countries, no way to join the adventitious cells to the mother cell. The Soviet Union on the contrary is a framework in which any nation can be inserted: It could later incorporate a Chilean Republic in the same way as a Ukrainian Republic is already incorporated. This way of thinking is not opposed to Marxism; it is different, however, in that it gives the state the preponderant and definitive place that Hegel gave it. Man as defined by the Hegelian idea is not an individual, but the state. The individual has died in it, has been absorbed into the higher reality and into the service of the state; in a wider sense, the "statesman" is the sea into which flows the river of history. Insofar as he participates in the state, man leaves both animality and individuality behind him: He is no longer separate from universal reality. Every isolable part of the world refers to the totality, but the supreme authority of the world state can only refer to itself. This conception, which is quite contrary to the popular reality of communism and far removed from activist enthusiasm, is an obvious paradox, but it is interesting for the way it underscores the relative meaninglessness and poverty of the individual reserve. One cannot miss the occasion to place the human individual in a position other than ultimate end and to liberate him by showing him a less narrow horizon. What we know of Soviet life relates to the limitations on enterprise and to the restrictions of personal freedom, but our habits are turned upside down in it and in any case what it calls into question goes beyond the narrow perspectives to which we willingly confine ourselves.

It is of course inevitable that the presence — and the threat — of the USSR cause diverse reactions. Mere rejection and hatred smack of negligence. In this instance, the courage to prefer the silence of thought, contempt for a failed organization and hatred for the barriers put in the way of people, lead one to desire a hard and decisive test. Like the devout believer who accepts the worst ahead of time, but whose prayer lays siege to heaven, some wait resignedly for the *détente*, for a less intractable attitude, but remain faithful to the cause that appeared to them to be compatible with a peaceful evolution of the world. Others find it difficult to imagine this world completely subjugated through an expansion of the Soviet Union, but the tension the latter maintains seems to imply the necessity of an economic transformation. In reality, a wonderful mental chaos comes from the action of Bolshevism in the world, and from the passivity, the moral nonexistence, that it encountered. But history is perhaps the only thing capable of putting an end to such chaos, through some military decision. We can only propose to seek the nature of that action of Bolshevism, which upsets the established order under our very eyes, much more thoroughly than Hitler managed to do.

The Working-Class Movement Against Accumulation

The USSR can change the world directly: The forces it comprises can prevail over the American coalition.

It can also change it through the repercussions of its action: The combat directed against it would bring its enemies to change the juridical foundations of their economy.

At all events, unless a total catastrophe occurs, a change of social structure is necessitated by a very rapid development of the productive forces, which the current regression of Europe is slackening only for a time.

The precise solution to which our troubles will lead may have only a secondary meaning for us. But we can become aware of the nature of the forces involved.

Undoubtedly the most consequential change in the disposal of excess resources was their allocation mainly to the development of capital equipment; it opened the industrial era and it remains the basis of the capitalist economy. What is called "accumulation" signifies that a number of wealthy individuals declined to engage in the unproductive expenditures of an ostentatious life-style and employed their available funds for the purchase of means of production. Whence the possibility of an accelerating development and even, as this development occurred, the allocation of a part of the increased resources to nonproductive expenditures.

In the last analysis, the working-class movement itself bears essentially on this problem of the distribution of wealth in contrary ways. What is the deeper significance of the strikes, the struggles of wage earners for increased wages and the reduction of labor

time? The success of workers' claims augments the çost of production and reduces not only the share reserved for the luxury
of the bosses, but that reserved for accumulation. One hour of
labor less and an increase in the cost of hourly labor, which the
growth of resources has made possible, show up in the distribution of wealth: If the worker had worked more and earned less, a
larger quantity of capitalist profit could have been used for the
development of the productive forces. Social security greatly
increases this effect in turn. In this way, the working-class movement and left-wing politics, which are at least liberal toward
wage earners, mainly signify, in opposition to capitalism, a greater
share of wealth devoted to nonproductive expenditure. True, this
allocation does not have some shining value as its aim: It merely
tends to give man a greater disposal of himself. The share allotted to present satisfaction is nonetheless increased at the expense
of the share allotted to the concern for an improving future. This
is why the left that we are familiar with generally conveys a sense,
if not of looseness, of relaxation; the right, a sense of tightness,
of parsimonious calculation. In theory the progressive parties
are animated by a generous movement and a fondness for living
without delay.

The Inability of the Czars to Accumulate
and Communist Accumulation

The economic development of Russia has differed profoundly from
ours and the considerations I have introduced cannot be applied
to it. Even in the West, the left-wing movements did not at first
have the meaning that I said. The French Revolution resulted in
a reduction of the sumptuary expenditures of the court and the
nobles on behalf of industrial accumulation. The revolution of
1789 remedied the backwardness of the French bourgeoisie relative to English capitalism. It was much later, when the left no

longer opposed a squandering nobility, but rather an industrial bourgeoisie, that it became generous without maintaining a great reserve. Now, the czarist Russia of 1917 was not very different from the France of the Ancien Régime; it was dominated by a class that was incapable of accumulating. The inexhaustible resources of a vast territory were unexploited for want of capital. It was only at the end of the nineteenth century that an industry of some scale developed. Moreover, the industry that did develop was overly dependent on foreign capital. "In 1934, only 53% of the funds invested in this industry were Russian."[1] And this development was so inadequate that, in almost every branch, the Russian inferiority increased yearly in relation to countries like France or Germany: "We are falling further and further behind," wrote Lenin.[2]

Under these conditions, the revolutionary struggle against the czars and landowners — from the democratic party (K.D.) to the Bolsheviks — for a very short time was propelled, as in a whirlpool, by the same set of complex movements that in France occupied the period from 1789 until recently. But its economic principles predetermined the direction it was to take: It could only put an end to nonproductive spending and reserve the resources for equipping the country. It was bound to have a goal opposed to that aimed for naturally, in the industrialized states, by the working masses and the parties that supported them. It was necessary to reduce those nonproductive expenditures for the benefit of accumulation. No doubt the reduction would affect the propertied classes, but the share that was levied in this way could not, or not primarily, be used to improve the lot of the workers; it had to be devoted above all to industrial equipment.

The First World War showed from the outset, in Russia, that when the combinations of industrial forces that constitute nations increase on all sides, none of them can stay behind. The Second World War completed the demonstration. While the development of the leading industrial countries was determined from within, it was mainly determined from the outside in the case of one backward country. Whatever one may say of the internal necessity for Russia to exploit industrially its resources, it needs to be added that in any case only that exploitation enabled it to overcome the ordeal of the recent war. The Russia of 1917, ruled by men who lived day to day, could survive only on one condition: It must develop its potential. To do so, it called on the leadership of a class that despised ostentatious squandering. The contribution of foreign capitalism and the increasing lag in Russia's industrial development are clear indications that the Russian bourgeoisie did not have the quantitative importance nor the ascendant character that would have enabled it to prevail. Whence the paradox of a proletariat forced to impose its will inflexibly on itself, to renounce life in order to make life possible. A parsimonious bourgeois foregoes the vainest luxury, but he nevertheless enjoys well-being; by contrast, the worker's renunciation took place under conditions of destitution.

"No one," wrote Leroy-Beaulieu, "can suffer like a Russian; no one can die like a Russian." But this extreme endurance appears very different from a calculation. It seems that in no other area of Europe was man so ignorant of the rational virtues of bourgeois life. These virtues require conditions of security: A capitalist speculation requires a rigorously established order, where it is possible to see ahead of one. Long being exposed to the incursions of barbarians over vast flat expanses, haunted by the specter of hunger and cold,[3] Russian life gave rise instead to the contrary virtues of insouciance, toughness and living in the present. A Soviet worker's renunciation of immediate advantage for a future good demanded that trust be placed in third parties. And not only that: He must also yield to constraint. Necessary efforts had to respond to strong and immediate incentives: Originally these were given in the nature of a dangerous, poor and immense land; they were to remain commensurate with that immensity and that poverty.

The men who, at the head of the proletariat, responded *without financial means* to the necessity of industrializing Russia could not in any case have the calm and calculating mind that presides over the capitalist enterprise. By virtue of the revolution they had made and the country in which they were born, they belonged entirely to the world of war. Being a mixture of terror and ardor, with the military code on one side and the flag on the other, this world was generally opposed to that of industry, to the cold composition of interests. Pre-soviet Russia had a basically agricultural economy dominated by the needs of the army, where the use of resources was more or less limited to squander and warfare. The army benefited only slightly from the industrial contribution, which is given to it unsparingly in other countries. The abrupt leap from czarism to communism meant that the allocation of resources to equipment could not be carried out as it was elsewhere, independently of the incentive constituted by the brutal necessity of war. Capitalist saving takes place in a sort of calm reserve, sheltered from the gales that intoxicate or terrify: Relatively speaking, the rich bourgeois is fearless and dispassionate. The Bolshevik leader on the contrary belonged, like the czarist proprietor, to the world of fear and passion. But, like the capitalist of the first period, he was opposed to wasteful spending. What is more, he shared these traits with every Russian worker, differing from the worker only to the slight extent that, in warlike tribes, a chief stands apart from those he commands. On this point the moral identity, at the outset, of the Bolshevik leaders and the working class is undeniable.

What is remarkable about this way of doing things is, in a certain sense, the holding of all of life under the sway of the present interest. Subsequent results are doubtless the justification for labor, but they are invoked to inspire self-sacrifice, enthusi-asm and passion; and similarly, threats have the acuity of an irra-tional contagion of fear. This is only one part of the picture, but a part on which the emphasis is placed. Under these conditions, the disparity between the value of the labor furnished by the work-ers and that of the wages distributed to them can be considerable.

In 1938, "the production total to be reached was set at 184 billion rubles, of which 114.5 billion were reserved for the pro-duction of the means of production and only 64 billion for that of objects of consumption."[4] This proportion does not exactly correspond to the disparity between wages and labor, yet it is evi-dent that the objects of consumption to be distributed, which first had to enter into the remuneration of the labor that was used to produce them, could not pay for more than a small part of the total labor. The disparity has tended to decrease since the war, but heavy industry has kept its privileged place. The man in charge of state planning, Voznessenski, admitted this on March 15, 1946: "The rhythm of production of the means of production envisaged by the plan," he said, "is somewhat greater than that of the pro-duction of objects of consumption."[5]

The Russian economy assumed its current form as early as 1929, at the beginning of the five-year plan.It is characterized by the allocation of nearly all the excess resources to production of the means of production. Capitalism was the first system to employ a substantial share of the available resources for that purpose, but there was nothing within it that opposed the freedom of squan-der (the reduced squander remained free, and moreover its occur-rence could be advantageous to capitalism). Soviet communism closed itself firmly to the principle of nonproductive expendi-ture. It did not do away with the latter by any means, but the social transformation it brought about eliminated the most costly forms of such spending and its incessant action tends to demand the maximum productivity from each individual, at the limit of human powers. No previous form of economy was able to reserve such a large share of the excess available resources for the increase of the productive forces, that is, for the growth of the system. In every social organization, as in every living organism, the surplus is distributed between the growth of the system and pure expenditure, of no use either to the maintenance of life or to growth. But the very nation that had almost perished from its inability to reserve a large enough share for growth, by a sudden inversion of its equilibrium reduced to a minimum the share that used to be given over to luxury and inertia: Today it only lives for the limitless growth of its productive forces.

We know that after having left Russia where he was an engineer and a party member, Victor Kravchenko published in the United States "sensational" memoirs in which he vehemently denounces the regime.[6] Whatever the value of Kravchenko's attacks, this description of Russian industrial activity offers a haunting vision of a world absorbed in a gigantic project. The author disputes the value of the means employed. There is no doubt that they were very harsh: Around 1937, the repression was ruthless, the deportation frequent; the results announced were sometimes only a façade for propaganda purposes; a portion of the wasted labor was due to disorder; and the control of a police that saw sabotage and opposition everywhere tended to demoralize the leadership and hinder production. These failings are well known from other sources (there was even a subsequent tendency to denounce the *purges* of that period as being too severe): We are only uninformed of their importance and there is no sufficiently reliable testimony that gives precise details. But Kravchenko's accusations cannot be cited against the substance of his testimony.

An immense machinery was assembled in which individual will was minimized with a view to the greatest output. No room was left for whimsy. The worker in this machinery received a labor pass-book and from that moment onward he could not move from one town or factory to another. A worker 20 minutes late could be sentenced to forced labor. An industrial manager, or military leader, could be sent without argument to some forsaken place in Siberia. The very example of Kravchenko reveals the essence of a world in which the only possibility is labor: the construction of a gigantic industry for the benefit of a future time. In such a world, passion, be it happy or sad, is only a brief episode, leaving few traces in memory. Political despair and the necessity of silence complete the picture: In the end, all of one's waking hours are dedicated to the fever of work.

On every side, amid the grinding of teeth and the songs, the heavy silence or the noise of the speeches, the poverty and the exaltation, day after day an enormous labor force, which the czars left powerless, constructs the edifice in which the usable wealth accumulates and multiplies.

The "Collectivization" of Lands

This same reductive effort was brought to bear on the countryside. However, the collectivization of lands is in theory the most questionable part of the changes in economic structure. There is no doubt that it cost dearly; indeed, it is regarded as the cruelest moment of an endeavor that was never mild. But if one judges this development of Russian resources in a general way, one risks forgetting the conditions in which it was begun and the necessity that compelled it. One fails to understand the urgency of a liquidation that did not target rich landowners, but rather the class of kulaks, whose standard of living was scarcely higher than that of poor peasants. It would have been wise, it seems, not to upset agriculture just as an industrial task was being undertaken that demanded the mobilization of every resource. It is difficult to judge from so far away, but the following explanation cannot be dismissed without good reason.

At the start of the first five-year plan it was necessary to provide for *real* compensation for the agricultural products that the workers would consume. Since the plan had to neglect light industry for heavy industry from the beginning, it was hard to envisage supplying the small objects needed by the farmers on a substantial scale. However, it was feasible to sell them tractors, the supplying of which was all the more in keeping with the plan because the plants that produced them would also serve to manufacture war machines if the need arose. But the small holdings of the kulaks had no use for tractors. Whence the necessity of replacing their private enterprises with much larger ones entrusted to associated peasants. (Moreover, the necessary and verifiable accounting of these collective farms facilitated requisitioning; without the latter, the peasants' consumption could not have been regulated according to a plan that tended to reduce the share of consumable goods across the board. And everyone is aware of the major obstacle to requisitions posed by small enterprises.)

These considerations had all the more force since industrialization always demands a large displacement of the population to the cities. If industrialization is slow, the displacement occurs of itself in a balanced way. Agricultural mechanization makes up for the depopulation of the rural areas. But a sudden development creates a call for manpower to which the response cannot long be delayed. Only agrarian "collectivism," coupled with mechanization, could ensure the maintenance and growth of agricultural production; without them, the proliferation of factories would only have led to disequilibrium.

But this cannot, it is said, justify the cruelty with which the kulaks were treated.

It is necessary at this point to pose the question more fully.

The Weakness of the Criticism Against the
Rigors of Soviet Industrialization

In the peacetime world to which the French are accustomed, one no longer imagines that cruelty can seem unavoidable. But this world of ease has its limits. Beyond it, situations arise in which, wrongly or rightly, acts of cruelty, harming individuals, seem negligible in view of the misfortunes they are meant to avoid. If one considers in isolation the advantage that a manufacture of tractors has over that of simple implements, it is difficult to understand the executions and deportations whose victims are estimated by some to be in the millions. But one immediate interest can be the corollary of another whose vital character cannot be denied. Today it is easy to see that the Soviets organizing production were replying in advance to a question of life and death.

I do not mean to justify, but to understand; given that purpose, it seems superficial to me to dwell on horror. It is easy to affirm — for the simple reason that the repression was terrible and that one hates terror — that gentleness would have succeeded better. Kravchenko argues this in a haphazard fashion. He also says, without due consideration, that the leadership would have prepared more effectively for war using more humane methods. What Stalin obtained from the workers and peasants went against many particular interests and even, in a general way, against the immediate interest of each person. If my meaning is clear, one will not imagine that a unanimous population yielded without resistance to such a harsh renunciation. Kravchenko could only uphold his criticisms by demonstrating the failure of industrialization more concretely. He confines himself to statements concerning the disorder and the carelessness. The proof of the futility of the industrial achievements would follow from the humiliating defeats of 1941 and 1942. And yet the Red Army crushed the Wermacht. No doubt with the aid of lend-lease. But he lets this surprising sentence slip out: "The Stalingrad triumph was clinched before the great flow of lend-lease got started; but American and Allied help belongs immediately thereafter in the estimate."[7] Thus, in the decisive battle of the war it was Russian arms, it was the result of the industrial effort, that came into play. Moreover, testifying in Washington before the congressional committee charged with investigating anti-American activities, Kravchenko makes this no less surprising statement: "It has to be understood," he says, "that all the talk about the impossibility of manufacturing the atomic bomb in the USSR because of the lag in technical development of Russian industry compared with American or British industry is not only tiresome, but also dangerous, because it deceives public opinion."

Provided we do not adhere too closely to the aims of an anti-Stalinist propaganda, Kravchenko's work is quite interesting, but it is devoid of theoretical value. Insofar as it does not engage the reader's emotions, but his intelligence, the author's criticism is unsubstantial. Today it serves America, putting Americans on guard (in the statement to the investigating committee) against imagining that the Kremlin has given up its plans for world revolution; yet it denounces a movement toward counterrevolution in Stalinism. If it sees a political and economic problem in the current communist organization, it has only one response: Stalin and his associates are responsible for an inadmissible state of affairs. The implication is that other men and other methods would have succeeded where Stalin is supposed to have failed. In reality it evades the painful solution of the problem. Apparently the Soviet Union, and even, speaking more generally, Russia — owing to the czarist legacy — would not have been able to survive without a massive allocation of its resources to industrial equipment. Apparently, if this allocation had been even a little less rigorous, even a little less hard to bear than Stalin made it, Russia could have foundered. Of course these propositions cannot be established in an absolute way, but the appearance is convincing, and Kravchenko's work does not give the lie to it. On the contrary, it supplies evidence in support of that massive, rigorous and scarcely bearable allocation by showing its results: At Stalingrad, Russia saved itself by its own means.

It is no use dwelling earnestly on the factors of error, disorder and production shortfalls. These factors are undeniable and not denied by the regime itself, but however prevalent they were, a decisive result was achieved. The question of less onerous methods, of a more rational production, is the only one left standing. Some will say: If the czars had continued, the capitalist rise would have followed; others will speak of Menshevism; and the least foolish, of some other form of Bolshevism. But the czars and the ruling class on which they relied were like a leak — a crack — in a closed system; Menshevism calling for an ascendant bourgeoisie was a cry in the wilderness; and Trotskyism implies distrust toward the possibilities of "socialism in one country." It only remains for one to defend the greater effectiveness of a less callous Stalinism, foreseeing the effect of its actions, and depending on voluntary consent for the unity needed to operate a social machine! The truth is that we rebel against an inhuman hardness. And we would rather die than establish a reign of terror; but a single man can die, and an immense population is faced with no other possibility than life. The Russian world had to make up for the backwardness of czarist society and this was necessarily so painful, it demanded an effort so great, that the hard way — in every sense the most costly way — became its only solution. If we have the choice between that which appeals to us and that which increases our resources, it is always hard to give up our desire in exchange for future benefits. It may be easy if we are in good condition: Rational interest operates without hindrance. But if we are exhausted, only terror and exaltation keep us from going slack. Without a violent stimulant Russia could not have recovered. (France's current troubles under less unfavorable conditions show the extent of that necessity: From a material standpoint life during the Occupation was relatively easy due to the lack of accumulation – we will always find it very difficult to work for the future.) Stalinism worked as well as it could, but always roughly, with the elements of fear and hope that were present in a grave yet promising situation, full of open possibilities.

Furthermore, the critique of Stalinism failed when it tried to present the policy of the current leaders as an expression of the interests, if not of a class, at least of a group that is aloof from the masses. Neither the collectivization of lands nor the orientation of industrial plans corresponded to the interests of the leaders as a group having a different economic position. Even extremely hostile authors do not deny the qualities of Stalin's entourage. Kravchenko is clear about this, and he personally knew men at the Kremlin who were near the top: "I can attest, however, that the great majority of the leaders with whom I came in contact were able men who knew their business; dynamic men deeply devoted to the work in hand."[8] In about 1932, Boris Souvarine, who knew the Kremlin from the first period, replied to my question: "In your opinion what reason could Stalin have had for pushing himself forward as he did, and shoving aside all the others?" "Undoubtedly," Souvarine answered, "he believed he was the only one, after Lenin's death, who had the strength to carry out the revolution." Souvarine said this quite plainly, without a trace of irony. The fact is that Stalinist policy is the rigorous – very rigorous – response to an organized economic necessity, which actually calls for an extreme rigor.

The strangest thing is that it is judged to be terroristic and Thermidorian at the same time. There could not be a more artless testimony to the confusion that an inflexible attitude introduces in the minds of the opponents. The truth is that we hate terror and we readily attribute it to a reactionary politics. But the agreement between nationalism and Marxism responded no less directly than rampant industrialization to a question of life and death: Multitudes lacking conviction would not have been able to fight unanimously for the communist revolution. If the revolution had not linked its destiny to that of the nation, it would have had to consent to perish. On this point, W.H. Chamberlin recalls an incident that made a strong impression on him: "There had been a time when nationalism was contraband, almost counterrevolutionary. I remember sitting in the State Opera House in Moscow and waiting for the unfailing burst of applause that followed an aria in Moussorgsky's *Khovantshina*, that opera of old Russia. The aria was a prayer that God would send some bright spirit to save '*Rus*' (the old name for Russia). The applause was the nearest thing to a demonstration against the Soviet regime...."[9] With the war approaching, it would not have been reasonable to ignore such deep reactions, but is it necessary to infer the abandonment of the internationalist principle of Marxism? The reports of the closed meetings of the Party Committee of the Sovnarkom (government of the Russian Federated Republic), given by Kravchenko, leave little room for doubt.[10] Within the Kremlin precincts, the party decision-makers spoke constantly of the "retreat from Leninism" as a "temporary tactical maneuver."

The Global Problem Versus the Russian Problem

One would have to blindfold oneself not to see in the Soviet Union of today, along with its harsh and intolerant aspects, the expression, not of a decadence, but of a terrific tension, a determination that has not drawn back and will not draw back from anything in order to solve the *real* problems of the Revolution. It is possible to offer "moral" criticisms against the facts, stressing that which, in reality, departs from the "ideal" of socialism that the Soviet Union once affirmed, from the notion of individual interests and individual thought. These conditions, however, are those of the USSR — not those of the entire world — and one would also have to cover one's eyes in order not to see the consequences of a *real* opposition between the doctrine and methods of the Soviets (tied to circumstances peculiar to Russia) and the economic problems of other countries.

In a fundamental way, the current system of the USSR, being geared to producing the means of production, runs counter to the workers' movements of other countries, the effect of which tends to reduce the production of capital equipment, increasing that of objects of consumption. But, at least on the whole, these workers' movements are responding to the economic necessity that conditions them just as the Soviet apparatus is responding to its own. The world economic situation is in fact dominated by the development of American industry, that is, by an abundance of the means of production and of the means for increasing them. The United States even has, in theory, the capacity to eventually place the industries of its allies in conditions approximating its own. Thus in the old industrial nations (in spite of current contrary aspects), the economic problem is becoming a problem not of outlets (already to a large extent questions of outlets have no possible answer), but of consumption of profits without compensation. It is doubtful that the juridical basis of production can be maintained. In any case, the present world calls for rapid changes on all sides. Never before was the earth animated by anything like this multiplicity of virtiginous movements. Of course, neither did the horizon ever appear to threaten such great and sudden catastrophes. Should it be said? If they come to pass, only the methods of the USSR would — in a wondrous silence of the individual

167

voice! – be equal to a ruined immensity. (Indeed, it may be that, in some obscure way, mankind aspires to build on just such a complete negation of niggardly disorder.) But, without manifesting more fear – since death soon puts an end to intolerable suffering – it is time to come back to this world and to take note of its increased possibilities. Nothing is closed to anyone who simply recognizes the material conditions of thought. On all sides and in every way, the world invites man to change it. Doubtless man on this side is not necessarily bound to follow the imperious ways of the USSR. For the most part, he is exhausting himself in the sterility of a fearful anticommunism. But if he has his own problems to solve, he has more important things to do than blindly to anathematize, than to complain of a distress caused by his manifold contradictions. Let him try to understand, or better, let him admire the cruel energy of those who broke the Russian ground; he will be closer to the tasks that await him. For, *on all sides and in every way, a world in motion wants to be changed.*

The Marshall Plan

The Threat of War

Apart from the communist enterprise and doctrine, the human mind accepts uncertainty and is satisfied with shortsightedness. Outside the Soviet world, there is nothing that has the value of an ascendant movement, nothing advances with any vigor. There persists a powerless dissonance of moans, of things already heard, of bold testimony to resolute incomprehension. This disorder is more favorable no doubt to the birth of an authentic *self-consciousness* than is its opposite, and one might even say that without this powerlessness – and without the tension that is maintained by communism's aggressiveness – consciousness would not be free, would not be *alert*.

In truth, the situation is painful and certainly of a nature to bring individuals out of their apathy. A "schism," a complete rift, divides not just minds, but the mind in general, for between the parties in question everything is originally in common. The division and the hatred are nonetheless complete and what they portend, it appears, is war: an inexpiable war, ineluctably the cruelest and most costly in history.

Moreover, reflection at the threshold of war is subject to singular conditions: Indeed, however one manages it, one cannot imagine – assuming it takes place – pursuing it beyond a conflagration.

What would be the meaning, in the event of a Russian victory, of a world generally ruined, where the United States, far from assisting other countries, would be more completely devastated than Germany today? The USSR would then also be ravaged, and the Marxism that would be established in the world would bear no resemblance to the one demanded by the development of productive forces. What would be the meaning of a destruction of capitalism that would be at the same time the destruction of capitalism's achievements? Obviously it would be the crudest possible denial of Marx's lucidity. The humanity that would have destroyed the work of the industrial revolution would be the poorest of all time; the memory of the recent wealth would finish the job of making that humanity unbearable. Lenin defined socialism as "the soviets, plus electrification." As a matter of fact, socialism does not just require the power of the people, but wealth as well. And no reasonable person can imagine it based on a world in which shanty towns would take the place of the civilization symbolized by the names of New York and London. That civilization is perhaps detestable; it sometimes seems to be only a bad dream; and there is no question that it generates the boredom and irritation that favor a slide toward catastrophe. But no one can reasonably consider something that only has the attraction of unreason in its favor.

Of course, one still has the option of imagining a victory of the United States over Russia that would not devastate the world so completely. But the "schism" would not be reduced for the fact that the victory was won at little cost to the victor. Apparently world dominion would then belong to the single holder of the decisive weapons, *but in the way that the victim belongs to the executioner.* This executioner's burden is so unenviable, the awareness that such a bloody solution would certainly poison social life is so strong, there there does not exist, on the American side, any substantial opinion in favor of war in the near future. Hence it is clear, or at least probable, that time is on the side of Russia.

The Possibility of a Nonmilitary Competition
Between Methods of Production

If one envisages, on the one hand, the silence of communism universally imposed by concentration camps, and, on the other, *freedom* exterminating the communists, there can be no remaining doubt: The situation could hardly be better for an awakening of the mind.

But while it is the result of menace, and though it was once linked to the feeling of a useless effort, of the game already lost, the alert consciousness cannot in any way surrender to anguish; it is dominated rather by the assurance of the moment (the laughable idea that darkness alone will be the answer to the will to see). But, up to the last, it will not be able to give up the *tranquil* pursuit of *good fortune*. It will give up only in the happy event of death.

In this situation of absolute schism, what prevents one from believing war to be inevitable is the idea that under the present conditions "the economy," to alter Clausewitz's phrase, might "continue it by other means."

The conflict that is engaged in the economic sphere opposes the world of industrial development – of nascent accumulation – to that of developed industry.

In a fundamental sense, it is from the side of exuberant production that the danger of war comes: If exportation is difficult, *and if no other outlet is open*, only war can be the client of a plethoric industry. The American economy is in fact the greatest explosive mass the world has ever known. True, its explosive pressure is not favored as it was in Germany, both externally by the proximity of dense military populations and internally by a disequilibrium between the different parts of the development of the productive forces. In return, the idea that that enormous machinery, driven by an *inevitable* movement of growth, is viable — balanced and rational — implies all the dangers of thoughtlessness. The fact that it was discharged in two world wars is not especially reassuring. In any case it is painful to see a dynamic society given over unreservedly and without long-range plans to the movement that propels it. It is painful to know that it is largely unacquainted with the laws of its development and that it produces without assessing the consequences of the production. This economy was capable of two wars; assuming its movement of growth continues, what sudden spell might make it capable of peace? Those who keep it running are naively convinced of having no other purpose. But should they not be asked whether they are not unconsciously pursuing the opposite of what their consciousness admits? The Americans are used to seeing others start wars, and experience has shown them the advantage of waiting.

To this pessimistic way of looking at things, however, it is necessary to oppose a clear view, based on the idea of a vast project whose realization has begun. While it is true that it is hard to imagine the United States prospering for long without the aid of a hecatomb of riches, in the form of airplanes, bombs and other military equipment, one can conceive of an equivalent hecatomb devoted to nonlethal works. In other words, if war is necessary to the American economy, it does not follow that war has to hold to the traditional form. Indeed, one easily imagines, coming from across the Atlantic, a resolute movement refusing to follow the routine: A conflict is not necessarily military; one can envisage a vast economic competition, which, for the competitor with the initiative, would cost sacrifices comparable to those of war, and which, from a budget of the same scale as war budgets, would involve expenditures that would not be compensated by any hope of capitalist profit. What I have said concerning the inertia of the

Western world requires at least this one qualification: There does not exist in that world either a political current (in the sense of propaganda) or an intellectual movement that reacts, but there is a specific determination that is responding to the Soviet pressure. The Marshall Plan is an isolated reaction, to be sure; it is the only undertaking that results from a systematic view opposing the Kremlin's will to world domination. The Marshall Plan succeeds in giving a clear focus to the current conflict: It is not essentially the struggle of two military powers for hegemony; it is the struggle of two economic methods. The Marshall Plan offers an organization of surplus against the accumulation of the Stalin plans. This does not necessarily imply armed struggle, which cannot lead to a real decision. If the opposed forces are different in nature economically, they must enter into competition on the plane of economic organization. This is what the Marshall Plan accomplishes, it would seem, as the West's only reaction to the movement of the Soviets in the world.

The Marshall Plan

One of the most original French economists, François Perroux, sees the Marshall Plan as a historical event of exceptional importance.[11] In his judgment, the Marshall Plan "begins the greatest economic experiment on an international scale that has ever been attempted" (p. 82). And its consequences, "on the global scale," are "bound to go far beyond the boldest and most promising structural reforms advocated by the various workers' parties on the national level" (p. 84). Moreover, it would constitute a veritable revolution, indeed, "*the* revolution that matters in this season of History" (p. 38). In fact, "the revolutionary transformation" it initiates changes "the customary relations between nations" (p. 184). For "there is more revolutionary spirit in averting the struggles of nations than in preparing for them in the name of class struggle" (p. 34). Thus, from the day that General Marshall's undertaking "would be crowned with a beginning of success, it would eclipse, in its benefits, the most thoroughgoing and least unsuccessful of the social revolutions" (p. 38).

This opinion is based on specific considerations. The Marshall Plan is intended to remedy the balance of payments deficit of the European nations vis-à-vis the United States. As a matter of fact, the deficit is old. "The exportation surplus characterizes the inveterate behavior of the balance of payments of the United States. From 1919 to 1935 it rose to a total of thirty billion four hundred and fifty million dollars..." (p. 215). But for the most part it was offset by gold payments, and the remainder was covered by a proven credit, pegged to the calculable interest. These resources are no longer available. Europe's poverty has given a very urgent character to the need for American products, and the latter's importation necessarily leads to an increased deficit, but there is no means of compensating for it. Not only gold and credit, but European holdings in the United States have dissipated. Tourism is just beginning to revive, and the partial destruction of the European merchant fleet has resulted in increased spending in dollars. Further, the disappearance of an intense trade with such areas as Southeast Asia, whose shipments to the United States were sizeable, deprives Europe of one of the means it had of mitigating its excess of American imports. As a result, the logic of commercial activity, which subordinates delivery to the profit of the supplier, would have made it impossible for a ruined Europe to return to a viable political economy.

But what would have been the sense of so great a disequilibrium in today's world? The United States was confronted with this problem. It was necessary either to adhere blindly to the principle of profit, but bear the consequences of an intolerable situation (it is easy to imagine the fate of America abandoning the rest of the world to hatred) or to give up the rule on which the capitalist world is based. It was necessary to deliver goods without payment: It was necessary to *give away* the product of labor.

The Marshall Plan is the solution to the problem. It is the only way to transfer to Europe the products without which the world's fever would rise.

François Perroux may be right to stress its importance. In the full sense of the word, it is perhaps not a *revolution*. But to say that the revolutionary significance of the Marshall Plan is doubtful would in any case be an imprecise remark. One can more simply ask whether it has the technical meaning, and the far-reaching political significance, that the author assigns to it. In developing this work, he does not take account of the plan's integration into the political game that opposes America and the USSR throughout the world. He confines himself to considering the quite new economic principles that it brings into the relations between nations. He does not consider the evolution of these relations due to the real, political implementation of the plan, nor the effects of this evolution on the international situation.

I will return to a question that the author has deliberately left open. But it is first necessary to show the interest of his technical analysis.

The Opposition Between "General" Operations and "Classical" Economy

François Perroux starts from the Bretton Woods agreements – and from their failure. He has no trouble showing that at Bretton Woods nothing of importance was considered that was not consistent with the rules of "classical economy." By this, he means "that general doctrine" which "is not found in its rigor in any of the classical English economists of the eighteenth century," but which "springs from them and follows its course, in unbroken meanders, from Adam Smith to A. C. Pigou."[12] For the classical economists the rational and normal use of resources "proceeds from *isolated* calculations."[13] These calculations "are the work of firms" and "as a rule exclude the transactions that proceed from, or result in, a grouping." In other words, the lender and the borrower view the transactions "each in terms of his own interest and without considering the repercussions on his neighbors" (p. 97). Under these conditions, the transactions remain unconnected with any *general* interest whatever; thus, political ends and group interests are not taken into account. The only things worth considering are the costs, the yield and the risks. There is in fact no other law than the profit of the isolated entities, of the firms involved in the transactions. Credit is granted insofar as the calculable interest of the creditor can be demonstrated to him. Now, the International Bank for Reconstruction and Economic Development restricted itself to principles defined in this way. "Instead of superimposing on the anarchy of individual loans a coherent and coordinated investment based on general calculations, it aims to perpetuate the old ways of distributing international credit, as a function of individual initiatives" (p. 155). Doubtless, "by its very existence, the International Bank constitutes a first attempt at bringing about, if not a grouping of needs, at least a grouping of parties destined to negotiate loan agreements among themselves" (p. 156). But a statutory clause "obliges it to study each demand *one by one*, considering the demand's particular advantage alone, without correlation to the ensemble formed by the aggregate of needs or even by the aggregate of demands actually formulated" (p. 155).

It could be said in short that the Bretton Woods agreements gave a precise definition to the impasse of the international economy. Established within the limits of the capitalist world, according to the rule of *isolated* profit — without which no trans-

action is conceivable[14] — it had to renounce its founding principles, or, in order to maintain them, renounce the conditions
without which it could not continue to exist. The inadequacy
of the International Bank and the Monetary Fund presented a negative version of the Marshall Plan's positive initiative.

It is the paradox of the capitalist economy that it is oblivious
to general ends, which give it its meaning and value, and that it
is never able to go beyond the limits of the isolated end. Further
on, I will show that a basic error of perspective results from this:
Our view of general ends is a reflection of isolated ends. But without making too hasty a judgment of the practical consequences,
it is very interesting to observe this sudden passage from one world
to another, from the primacy of the *isolated* interest to that of the
general interest.

François Perroux has very rightly drawn a definition of the Marshall Plan from this fundamental opposition: It is, he says, "an
investment in the world's interest" (p. 160).

In this operation, "the nature and scale of the risks run, the
size and fate of the stakes involved would make calculations of
net interest illusory." The operation "was prepared, decided, and
will be conducted on the basis of political options and macro-
scopic calculations which classical analysis does not really help
us to understand" (pp. 172–73). Henceforth, "the demands for and
distribution of credit depend on collective calculations that have
no relation to the isolated calculations on which liberalism liked
to dwell" (pp. 99–100). There is a "collective supply, meeting a
collective demand." Of course, "this grouping of supplies and
demands is in obvious contrast with the classical doctrine and practice of investment" (p. 167).

The economic ensembles, the states, that are integrated into
the global operation are led to change over from the primacy of
their *isolated* interest to the interest of regional understandings.

The protectionism of industries, maintained out of ignorance, or in negation of the neighbors' interests, is replaced by the need for systematic agreements with a view to the distribution of labor. But the regional understanding is itself only a stage in world integration. There is no isolated entity aware only of itself and the world – or the state in a world dominated by the economy – but a generalized contesting of isolation. The very movement that "makes it depend on its neighbors" integrates each economy into the world (p. 110).

Under these conditions, "the distribution of credit has ceased to be a *profession* and has become a *function*" (p. 157). One might say more precisely that mankind considered in general would use credit for ends it would decide on without any longer having to serve the interest of that credit, without having to stay within the limits defined by the creditor's interest. Mankind embodied in a manager, an administrator of the E.C.A. (Economic Cooperation Administration) would share the investment through constant negotiations, according to a basic law that is the negation of the rule of profit. The old expression of this new law is familiar. An operation in the interest of the world is necessarily based on this unquestionable principle: "From each according to his abilities, to each according to his needs."

From the "General" Interest According to François Perroux to the Perspective of "General Economy"

However bizarre and out of place (in every sense) communism's basic formula may be in this connection, for the Marshall Plan – a logical "investment in the world's interest," or even a failed attempt at such an ideal operation – no other formula will do. Needless to say, a goal *aimed for* is not a goal *reached*, but, consciously or not, the plan cannot aim for any other goal.

Obviously this cannot help but bring in numerous difficulties.

François Perroux is no doubt aware of these, but he does not consider them, at least not within the limits of his short book.

He intentionally overlooks the aleatory character of the plan and our uncertainty as to its repercussions on general policy.

He also overlooks the fact that the plan implies a contribution to it. In short, it has to be financed. Depending on the nature of this contribution and the extent of the mobilizations, the effect of the plan may be limited, its meaning may be altered.

Here it may be useful, in order to study the quality of that contribution, to introduce, in a direction that extends that of François Perroux's work, a whole set of theoretical considerations. First of all, the plan implies a mobilization of capital and its exemption from the common law of profit. This capital will come, according to François Perroux's expression, from the reserves of "an internationally dominant economy." Indeed, this requires an economy so developed that the needs of growth are having a hard time absorbing its excess resources. It also demands a national income out of proportion with that of the other nations, so that a relatively small deduction from it will mean a relatively large amount of aid for the deficient economies. The contribution of five billion dollars is vitally important for Europe, but the sum is less than the cost of alcohol consumption in the United States in 1947. The amount in question roughly corresponds to three weeks of war expenditures. It is approximately 2 percent of the gross national product.

Without the Marshall Plan, this 2 percent could have gone in part to increase nonproductive consumption, but since it is chiefly a matter of durable goods, in theory it would have been used for the growth of the American forces of production, that is, for increasing the wealth of the United States. This is not necessarily shocking, and even if one is shocked, it appears that one must be so merely from a moral standpoint. Let us try to consider what it means *in a general sense*. This increase of wealth would have answered the combined demands of many *isolated* interests. Returning to the viewpoint of "general economy," beyond the general operations considered by François Perroux, *isolated* interest means precisely this: that each *isolated* entity on earth, in all of living nature, tends to grow and theoretically can do so. In fact every isolated living particle can use a surplus of resources – which it has at its disposal under average conditions – either for an increase through reproduction or for its individual growth. But this need to grow, to carry growth to the limits of possibility, is characteristic of *isolated* beings; it defines *isolated* interest. It is customary to consider *general* interest in terms of *isolated* interest, but the world is not so simple that one can always do this without introducing an error of perspective.

It is easy to make this error perceptible. Considered in the aggregate, the growth of living particles cannot be infinite. There exists a point of saturation of the space open to life. Doubtless the openness of space to the growth of active forces is liable to vary with the nature of the living forms. The wings of birds opened a more extensive space to growth. The same is true of human techniques that made possible successive leaps in the development of life systems, of systems that consume and produce energy. Each new technique itself enables a new growth of the productive forces. But this movement of growth runs up against limits at every stage of life. It is continually stopped and forced to wait for a change in the conditions of life before resuming. The cessation of development does not do away with the resources that could have increased the volume of life forces. But the energy that might have produced an increase is then expended to no purpose. As far as human activities are concerned, the resources that could have been accumulated (capitalized) as new forces of production are dissipated in one way or another. As a general rule, it has to be granted that life or wealth cannot be indefinitely *prolific* and that the moment always arrives when they must stop grow-ing and begin to spend. The intense proliferation of immortal liv-ing beings — the simplest beings — succeeds the luxury of death and sexual reproduction, which maintains an immense endemic squander. The eating of animals by one another is itself a brake on overall growth. And similarly, once domination of the avail-able space is ensured at the expense of animals, men have their wars and their thousand forms of useless consumption. Mankind is at the same time — through industry, which uses energy for the development of the forces of production — a manifold open-ing of the possibilities of growth and an infinite capacity for wasteful consumption.

But growth can be viewed in theory as the concern of the iso-lated individual, who does not measure its limits, who struggles painfully to ensure it, and who does not worry about its conse-quences. The formula for growth is that of the isolated lender: "each in his own interest and without considering the repercus-sions on one's neighbors," let alone the *general* repercussions. On the other hand, there exists (beyond the overall human interest which, conceived just as I have said, is only an aberrant multi-plication of the isolated interest) a *general* point of view, from which life is seen in a new light. Of course, this point of view does not imply a negation of the advantages of growth, but it opposes to individual blindness — and despair — a strange, exu-berant, simultaneously beneficent and disastrous sense of wealth. This interest is drawn from an experience contrary to that in which selfishness dominates. It is not the experience of the individual anxious to assert himself by developing his personal forces. It is the contrary awareness of the futility of anxiety. The themes of economics enable one to specify the nature of this interest. If one considers the holders of capital as a body, one quickly perceives the contradictory character of these interests. Each holder demands an interest from his capital, and this implies an unlimited development of the forces of production. What is blindly denied in the conception of these essentially productive operations is the sum —not unlimited but substantial – of products consumed wastefully. What is sadly forgotten in these calculations is, above all, that fabulous riches had to be dissipated in wars. This can be expressed more clearly by saying – paradoxically – that economic problems in which, as in "classical" economics, the question is limited to the pursuit of profit are *isolated* or *limited* problems; that in the *general* problem there always reappears the essence of the biomass, which must constantly destroy (consume) a surplus of energy.

Returning to the Marshall Plan, it is now easy to be precise. It contrasts with *isolated* operations of the "classical" type, but not through its grouping of collective supplies and demands; it is a general operation in that *in one respect* it is a renunciation of the growth of productive forces. It tends to solve a general problem in that it is an unsecured investment. At the same time, it nevertheless anticipates an ultimate utilization for growth (needless to say, the general point of view implies these two aspects at the same time), but it carries this possibility over to an area where destruction – and technological backwardness – has left the field open. In other words, its contribution is that of a condemned wealth.

By and large, there exists in the world an excess share of resources that cannot contribute to a growth for which the "space" (better, the possibility) is lacking. Neither the share that it is necessary to sacrifice, nor the moment of sacrifice are ever given exactly. But a *general* point of view requires that at an ill-defined time and place growth be abandoned, wealth negated, and its possible fecundation or its profitable investment ruled out.

Soviet Pressure and the Marshall Plan

In any case, a fundamental difficulty cannot be removed. How is the contribution to be set free? How can five billion dollars be withdrawn from the rule of isolated profit? How can it be sacrificed? This is where the plan's integration into the real political game becomes the question – which, as I have said, was not treated in Perroux's work. Everything would apparently have to be reconsidered starting from there. François Perroux has defined the plan as if the contribution's liberation from the common rule were given, as if it were the effect of the common interest. I have not been able to agree with him entirely on this point. The plan may be an "investment in the world's interest," but it also may be an investment "in America's interest." I do not say that this is the case, but the question arises. Moreover, it is possible that, being "in the world's interest" at the outset, it will be warped in the direction of the American interest.

Theoretically, it is a profound negation of capitalism; in this restricted sense, nothing is to be taken away from the opposition brought out in François Perroux's analysis. But in reality?

There is not yet a reality. Let us merely pose the question: It may be that in wanting to deny itself, capitalism will reveal at the same time that it could not avoid doing so and that it lacked the necessary strength for such self-denial. And yet, for the American world, it is a question of life and death.

This aspect of the modern world is overlooked by most of those who try to understand it: In a paradoxical way, the situation is governed by the fact that without the salutary fear of the Soviets (or some analogous threat), there would be no Marshall Plan. The truth is that the diplomacy of the Kremlin holds the key to the American coffers. Paradoxically, the tension it maintains in the world is what determines the latter's movements. Such assertions could easily slip into absurdity, but one can say that without the

USSR, without the politics of tension it adheres to, the capitalist world could not be certain of avoiding paralysis. This truth
dominates current developments.

It is not certain that the Soviet regime, at present, is answer-
ing the economic demands of the world in general. One at least
imagines that a plethoric economy does not necessarily require
the dictatorial organization of industry. But the *political action* of
the Union and the Cominform is necessary to the world economy.
Here the action is the consequence not only of a difference in
superstructures (in the juridical systems of production), but also
a difference in economic levels. In other words, the political
regime in one place, the Russian world, expresses the inequality
of resources (of the movement of energy) by an aggressive agitation, an extreme tension of the class struggle. It goes without
saying that this tension is favorable to a less unequal distribution
of resources, to a circulation of wealth that the increasing unevenness of levels paralyzed. The Marshall Plan is the consequence
of a working-class agitation that it tries to remedy with a rise in
the Western standard of living.

The communist opposition to the Marshall Plan itself prolongs
the initial setting in motion of the plan. It tends to impede the
plan's implementation, but contrary to appearances, it accentuates the very movement it combats. It accentuates and controls
it; in theory, aid to Europe introduces the possibility, indeed the
necessity, of an American intervention, but the Soviet opposition
makes any irregularity or excess difficult, reducing the risk that
the intervention might turn into a conquest. True, Soviet sabotage could diminish the effects of the plan. But on the other hand
it increases the feeling of necessity, if not of distress, that ensures
a less hesitant implementation.

One cannot overemphasize the importance of these movements
of repercussion. They go in the direction of a profound transfor-

mation of the economy. It is not certain that their results will suffice, but these paradoxical exchanges prove that the world's contradictions will not necessarily be resolved by war. In a general way, whether socialist or communist, the working-class agitation is actually conducive to a peaceful evolution — without revolution — of the economic institutions. A primary error is in thinking that a moderate, reformist agitation would ensure this evolution by itself. If the agitation that is due to the communist, revolutionary initiative did not take a threatening turn, there would be no more evolution. But one would be wrong to imagine that the only successful effect of communism would be the seizure of power. Even in prison, the communists would continue to "change the world." By itself, an effect such as the Marshall Plan is considerable, but it should not be seen as a limit. The economic competition resulting from subversive action could easily entail, beyond changes in the distribution of wealth, a deeper change in structures.

Where Only the Threat of War Can Still "Change the World"

From the outset, the Marshall Plan tends toward a raising of the standard of living world-wide. (It may even have the effect of raising the Soviet standard of living, at the expense of the growth of productive forces.) But under capitalist conditions the raising of the standard of living is not a sufficient relief from the continual growth of the productive forces. The Marshall Plan is also, from the start, a means *external to capitalism* of raising the standard of living. (In this respect, it does not matter whether the effect occurs outside of America.) Thus a shift begins toward a structure less different from that of the USSR, toward a relatively state-controlled economy, the only type possible where, the growth of productive forces being curbed, capitalist accumulation, and consequently profit, would no longer have a sufficient margin. Moreover, the form of aid to Europe is not the only indicator of a development that is generally favored by working-class agitation. The United States is struggling with insoluble contradictions. It defends free enterprise, but it thereby increases the importance of the state. It is only advancing, as slowly as it can, toward a point where the USSR rushed headlong.

The solving of social problems no longer depends on street uprisings, and we are far from the time when expanding populations, short of economic resources, were constrained to invade the wealthiest regions. (Besides, military conditions work in favor of the rich nowadays, the opposite being true in the past.) Hence the consequences of politics apart from wars are of utmost interest. We cannot be sure that they will save us from disaster; but they are our only chance. We cannot deny that war often precipitated the development of societies: Aside from the Soviet Union itself, our least rigid social relations, and our nationalized industries and services, are the result of two wars that shook Europe. It is even true that we come out of the last war with an increased population; living standards themselves are still improving overall. Nevertheless, it is hard to see what a third war would bring us, other than the irremediable reduction of the globe to the condition of Germany in 1945. Henceforth we need to think in terms of a peaceful evolution without which the destruction of capitalism would be at the same time the destruction of the *works* of capitalism, the cessation of economic development, and the dissipation of the socialist dream. We must now expect from the *threat* of war that which yesterday it would have been callous but correct to expect from war. This is not reassuring, but the choice is not given.

"Dynamic Peace"

We only need to bring a clear principle into political judgments.

If the threat of war causes the United States to commit the major part of the excess to military manufactures, it will be useless to still speak of a peaceful evolution: In actual fact, war is bound to occur. *Mankind will move peacefully toward a general resolution of its problems only if this threat causes the U.S. to assign a large share of the excess — deliberately and without return — to raising the global standard of living, economic activity thus giving the surplus energy produced an outlet other than war.* It is no longer a matter of saying that the lack of disarmament means war; but American policy hesitates between two paths: Either rearm Europe with the help of a new lend-lease, or use, at least partially, the Marshall Plan for equipping it militarily. Disarmament under the present conditions is a propaganda theme; by no means is it a way out. But if the Americans abandon the specific character of the Marshall Plan, the idea of using a large share of the surplus for nonmilitary ends, this surplus will explode exactly where they will have decided it would. At the moment of explosion it will be possible to say that the policy of the Soviets made the disaster inevitable. The consolation will be not only absurd but false as well. It needs to be stated, here and now, that, on the contrary, to leave war as the only outlet for the excess of forces produced is to accept responsibility for that result. It is true that the USSR is putting America through a difficult trial. But what would this world be like if the USSR were not there to wake it up, test it and force it to "change"?

I have presented the inescapable consequences of a precipitous armament, but this in no way argues for a disarmament, the very idea of which is unreal. A disarmament is so far from being a possibility that one cannot even imagine the effects it would have. To suggest that this world be given a rest is fatuous in the extreme. Rest and sleep could only be, at best, a preliminary to war. Only a *dynamic peace*[15] answers a crying need for change. It is the only formula that can be opposed to the revolutionary determination of the Soviets. And *dynamic peace* assumes that their resolute determination will maintain the threat of war; it means the arming of opposite camps.

Mankind's Accomplishment Linked to that of the American Economy

That said, it stands to reason that only a success of the American methods implies a peaceful evolution. It is to Albert Camus's great credit that he so clearly demonstrated the impossibility of a revolution without war, at least a classic revolution. But it is not necessary to see an inhuman will embodied in the USSR or the work of evil in the politics of the Kremlin. It is cruel to desire the continuation of a regime relying on a secret police, the muzzling of thought and numerous concentration camps. But there would be no Soviet camps in this world if an immense movement of human masses had not responded to a pressing need. It would be useless in any case to pretend to *self-consciousness* without perceiving the meaning, *the truth* and the crucial value of the tension maintained in the world by the USSR. (If this tension were to fail, a feeling of calm would be completely unwarranted; there would be more reason than ever to be afraid.) Anyone who lets himself be blinded by passion, so that he sees only excess in the USSR, commits himself to an equivalent excess in the sense of blindness: He gives up his claim to the complete lucidity through which man has the chance to be, finally, a *self-consciousness*. To be sure, *self-consciousness* is also ruled out within the limits of the Soviet sphere. Moreover, it cannot bind itself to anything that is already given. It implies, under the threat of war, a rapid change and the success of the world's dominant power.[16] On the other hand, it is already involved in a subsequent choice of the American democracy, and it cannot help but call for the latter's success without war. The national point of view is irrelevant.[17]

Consciousness of the Ultimate End of Wealth and "Self-Consciousness"

Doubtless it is paradoxical to tie a truth so intimate as that of *self-consciousness* (the return of being to full and irreducible sovereignty[18]) to these completely external determinations. Yet it is easy to perceive the deep meaning of these determinations – and of this entire book – if one returns to the essential without further delay.

In the first place, the paradox is carried to an extreme owing to the fact that politics considered in terms of "the dominant international economy" only aims at an improvement of the global standard of living.[19] It is in a sense disappointing and depressing. But it is the starting point and the basis, not the completion, of *self-consciousness*. This needs to be presented in a rather precise way.

If *self-consciousness* is essentially the full possession of intimacy, we must return to the fact that all possession of intimacy leads to a deception.[20] A sacrifice can only posit a sacred *thing*. The *sacred thing* externalizes intimacy: It makes visible on the outside that which is really within. This is why *self-consciousness* demands finally that, in connection with intimacy, nothing further can occur. This does not in any way involve an intention to eliminate what remains: Who would think of getting rid of the work of art or of poetry? But a *point* must be uncovered where dry lucidity coincides with a sense of the sacred. This implies the reduction of the sacred world to the component most purely opposed to *things*, its reduction to pure intimacy. This comes down in fact, as in the experience of the mystics, to intellectual contemplation, "without shape or form," as against the seductive appearances of "visions," divinities and myths. This means precisely, from the viewpoint introduced in this book, that one must decide in a fundamental debate.

The beings that we are are not given once and for all; they appear designed for an increase of their energy resources. They generally make this increase, beyond mere subsistence, their goal and their reason for being. But with this subordination to increase, the being in question loses its autonomy; it subordinates itself to what it will be in the future, owing to the increase of its resources. In reality, the increase should be situated in relation to the moment in which it will resolve into a pure expenditure. But this is precisely the difficult transition. In fact, it goes against consciousness in the sense that the latter tries to grasp some object of acquisition, *something*, not the *nothing* of pure expenditure. It is a question of arriving at the moment when consciousness will cease to be a consciousness of *something*; in other words, of becoming conscious of the decisive meaning of an instant in which increase (the acquisition of *something*) will resolve into expenditure; and this will be precisely *self-consciousness*, that is, a consciousness that henceforth has *nothing as its object*.[21]

This completion, linked — there where lucidity has its odds — to the easing associated with an upward adjustment of living standards, implies the value of a setting in place of social existence. In a sense, this *setting in place* would be comparable to the transition from animal to man (of which it would be, more precisely, the last act). It is as if, in this way of looking at things, the final goal were given. In the end, everything falls into place and takes up its assigned role. Today Truman would appear to be blindly preparing for the final — and secret — apotheosis.[22]

But that is obviously an illusion. More open, the mind discerns, instead of an antiquated teleology, the truth that silence alone does not betray.

190

Notes

Preface

1. This first volume will have a continuation. Further, it is being published in a collection that I direct, which intends to publish, among others, works in "general economy." [The second and third volumes of *The Accursed Share* are forthcoming from Zone Books.]

2. Here I must thank my friend Georges Ambrosino, research director of the X-Ray Laboratory, without whom I could not have constructed this book. Science is never the work of one man; it requires an exchange of views, a joint effort. This book is also in large part the work of Ambrosino. I personally regret that the atomic research in which he participates has removed him, for a time, from research in "general economy." I must express the hope that he will resume in particular the study he has begun with me of the movements of energy on the surface of the globe.

Part One

1. Of the materiality of the universe, which doubtless, in its proximate and remote aspects, is never anything but a beyond of thought. *Fulfillment* designates that which *fulfills itself*, not that which *is fulfilled*. *Infinite* is in opposition both to the limited determination and to the assigned *end*.

2. It is assumed that if industry cannot have an indefinite development, the same is not true of the "services" constituting what is called the tertiary sector

of the economy (the primary being agriculture and the secondary, industry), which includes specialized insurance organizations as well as the work of artists.

3. See pages 35-6.

4. Unfortunately, it is not possible to discuss all these problems within the framework of a first — theoretical and historical — essay.

5. See W. Vernadsky, *La Biosphère*, Paris, 1929, where some of the considerations that follow are outlined (from a different viewpoint).

6. The association is apparently implied in the expression, "the sin of the *flesh*."

PART TWO

1. Bernardino de Sahagún, *Historia general de las cosas de Nueva España*, Mexico City: Porrúa, 1956. Book VII, Ch. 2.

2. *Historia de los Mexicanos por sus pinturas*, Ch. 6.

3. Sahagún, Book II, Ch. 5.

4. *Ibid.*, appendix of Book II.

5. *Ibid.*, Book II, Ch. 24.

6. *Ibid.*, Book II, Ch. 5.

7. *Ibid.*, Book II, Ch. 24.

8. *Ibid.*, Book II, Ch. 21.

9. *Ibid.*, Book II, Ch. 34.

10. *Ibid.*, Book II, Ch. 36.

11. *Ibid.*, Book II, Ch. 33.

12. *Ibid.*, Book VI, Ch. 31.

13. *Ibid.*, Book VI, Ch. 3.

14. I am basing myself on the views of Marcel Granet and Georges Dumézil.

15. I wish to emphasize a basic fact: The separation of beings is limited to the real order. It is only if I remain attached to the order of *things* that the separation is *real*. It *is* in fact *real*, but what is real is *external*. "Intimately, all men are one."

16. In the simple sense of a knowledge of the *divine*. It has been said that the texts that I refer to show a Christian influence. This hypothesis seems pointless to me. The substance of Christian beliefs is itself drawn from the previous

religious experience and the world depicted by Sahagún's informants has a coherence all its own. If need be, the voluntary poverty of Nanauatzin could be interpreted as a Christianization. But this opinion appears to me to be based on a contempt for the Aztecs, which, it must be said, Sahagún seems not to have shared.

17. Sahagún, Book VII, Ch. 20.

18. *Ibid.*, Book IX, Ch. 4.

19. *Ibid.*, Book IX, Ch. 5.

20. *Ibid.*, Book IX, Ch. 6.

21. *Ibid.*, Book IX, Ch. 10.

22. *Ibid.*, Book IX, Ch. 7.

23. *Ibid.*, Book IX, Chs. 12 and 14.

24. These facts are drawn from the authoritative study by Marcel Mauss, *Essai sur le don: Forme et raison de l'échange dans les sociétés archaïques*, in the *Année sociologique*, 1923-24, pp. 30-186, translated as *The Gift: Forms and Functions of Exchange in Archaic Societies*. New York: Norton, 1967.

25. Let me indicate here that the studies whose results I am publishing here came out of my reading of the *Essai sur le don*. To begin with, reflection on potlatch led me to formulate the laws of *general economy*. But it may be of interest to mention a special difficulty that I was hard put to resolve. The general principles that I introduced, which enable one to interpret a large number of facts, left irreducible elements in the potlatch, which in my mind remained the origin of those facts. Potlatch cannot be unilaterally interpreted as a consumption of riches. It is only recently that I have been able to reduce the difficulty, and give the principles of "general economy" a rather ambiguous foundation. What it comes down to is that a squandering of energy is always the opposite of a thing, but it enters into consideration only once it has entered into the order of things, once it has been changed into a *thing*.

PART THREE

1. Emile Dermenghem, *Témoignages de l'Islam: Notes sur les valeurs permanentes et actuelles de la civilisation musulmane*, pp. 371-87.

2. *Ibid.*, p. 373.

3. Of course, Emile Dermenghem is well aware of this; further on he writes: "since Moslem means precisely 'resigned, submissive'..." (p. 381). Dermenghem's competence in Islamic matters is undeniable; he has written admirably concerning Moslem mysticism, and the only thing in question is his difficulty in trying to define the *abiding* values of Islam.

4. *Ibid.*, pp. 376-77.

5. Maurice Gaudefroy-Demombynes, *Les Institutions musulmanes*, Paris, 1946 (3rd ed.), p. 120.

6. *Ibid.*, p. 121.

7. *Ibid.*, pp. 121-22.

8. H. Holma, *Mahomet, prophète des Arabes*, 1946, p. 72.

9. See below, p. 106ff.

10. Henri Pérès devotes a remarkable article in the view *L'Islam et l'Occident* ("La poésie arabe d'Andalousie et ses relations possibles avec la poésie des troubadours," pp. 107-8) to the question of the Andalusian influence. According to the author, the question cannot be decided conclusively but the connections are quite pronounced. They concern not only the content, the basic themes, but also the form of the poetry. The coincidence of the great era of Arab poetry of Andalusia (eleventh century) and the birth of Provençal courtly poetry (end of the eleventh century) is striking. Further, the relations between the Spanish Moslem world and the Christian world of the North of Spain or France can be established precisely.

11. Sir Charles Bell, *Portrait of the Dalai Lama*, London, 1946.

12. However, for a long time the Moslem countries that arrived at an equilibrium, and enjoyed an urban civilization, were the prey of other Moslems who were still nomadic. The latter only urbanized after having overthrown the empire of the first conquerors.

13. See R. Grousset, *Bilan de l'histoire*, Paris: Plon, 1946: "A la source des invasions," pp. 273-99.

PART FOUR

1. His famous studies on "the Protestant ethic and the spirit of capitalism," *Die protestantische Ethik und der Geist des Kapitalismus*, first published in *Archiv für Socialwissenschaft und Socialpolitik*, vols. XX and XXI, 1904 and 1905, form the first volume of the *Religionssoziologie*, Tübingen, 1921, 3 vols.

2. R.H. Tawney, *Religion and the Rise of Capitalism* (2nd. ed.), New York, 1947.

3. *Ibid.*, p. xxvii, n. 11.

4. *Ibid.*, p. 99.

5. Quoted by Tawney, *Ibid.*, p. 105.

6. *Ibid.*, p. 112.

7. *Ibid.*, p. 109.

8. Everything that Tawney says about the repression of begging and vagrancy is quite remarkable (see p. 265). One rarely encounters a clearer perception of the action of economic interest on ideology. In this case, the brutality of a society bent on getting rid of *nonproductive* poverty found expression in the harshest forms of the authoritarian ethic. Even Bishop Berkeley suggested that "sturdy beggars should be seized and made slaves to the public for a certain term of years" (p. 270).

9. *Ibid.*, p. 113.

10. The only one, that is, by which one can go to the limits of the possible.

11. Here the medieval representation is only the closest form from which we are separated precisely by the Reformation and its economic consequences. But the ancient representations, the oriental representations, or the primitive representations have almost the same meaning, or a purer meaning, in our eyes.

12. It should be added: or of a raw material, indefinitely available for the use of the producer or merchant.

13. What I mean specifically is *aesthetic* action, motivated by feeling and seeking a sentimental satisfaction, wanting to do, in a word, that which cannot be *done*, but only experienced, received as grace is received in the Calvinist conception.

14. All working people furnished it; the mass furnished, with its own provisions, those of the workers who were employed at sumptuary tasks.

PART FIVE

1. Jorré, *L'U.R.S.S. La Terre et les Hommes*, Paris, 1945, p. 133.

2. *Ibid.*

3. *"Gholod i kholod"* in Russian.

4. Alexinsky, *La Russie révolutionnaire*, Paris, 1947, pp. 168-69.

5. *Ibid.*, p. 254.

6. V.A. Kravchenko, *I Chose Freedom*, 1946. The use that I have made of this important document, which is obviously biased but authentic, consists in drawing out some of the truthful information it contains, in keeping with strict critical rules. From its flagrant deficiencies, its contradictions, its superficialities, and, in general, from the author's lack of intellectual solidity, nothing can be concluded against the book's authenticity. It is a document like any other, to be used with caution, like any other document.

7. *Ibid.*, p. 403.

8. *Ibid.*, p. 400.

9. W.H. Chamberlin, *The Russian Engima*, New York, 1944, p. 278.

10. Kravchenko, pp. 421-26.

11. François Perroux, *Le Plan Marshall ou l'Europe nécessaire au monde*, Paris, 1948.

12. *Ibid.*, p. 127. The author specifies, a few lines later: "Thus *classical* here has about the same meaning that Keynes gives it in the first pages of the *General Theory*."

13. *Ibid.*, p. 130 (italics in the original).

14. The result of the transaction can be an absence of profit, or even a loss, as an effect that was not provided for in its *conception*. The principle is unalterable nonetheless.

15. To use the phrase coined by Jean-Jacques Servan-Schreiber. See *L'Occident face à la paix*, a series of remarkable articles published in *Le Monde* of January 15, 16, 17 and 18, 1949.

16. As Servan-Schreiber indicates, and as progressive American intellectuals tend to think, one can expect a considerable, rapid transformation of the internal situation of the United States from the swift rise of a new political force, that of the trade unions.

17. Why deny the fact that there can no longer be a true initiative toward independence on the part of countries other than the USSR or the USA? To lag behind no longer has any meaning except in day-to-day polemics.

18. Which is freedom in the moment, independent of a task needing to be carried out.

19. I do mean *global*: In this sense, the latest orientation of American policy, indicated in the "Truman Plan," is more meaningful than the Marshall Plan itself. It will seem foolish, of course, to see a solution of the problem of war in connection with these economic measures. In actual fact, even if they were implemented in a serious way, they would only eliminate the necessity, not the possibility, of war; but, with the help of the terrible threat of the current weapons, that might suffice in principle. In any case, nothing more could be done.

20. See above, Part IV, Ch. 2, "The Bourgeois World," p. 129.

21. Nothing but pure interiority, which is not a thing.

22. The moment would arrive when passion would no longer be an agent of unconsciousness. It will be said that only a madman could perceive such things in the Marshall and Truman plans. I am that madman. In the very precise sense that there is the choice of two things: Either the operation will fail, or the madman will arrive at the *self-consciousness* I speak of, because reason, being consciousness, is fully conscious only if it has for an object that which is not reducible to it. I apologize for introducing considerations here that refer to a precise fact: that in other respects the author of this book on economy is situated (by a part of his work) in the line of mystics of all times (but he is nonetheless far removed from all the presuppositions of the various mysticisms, to which he opposes only the lucidity of *self-consciousness*).

This edition designed by Bruce Mau
Type composed by Archie at Canadian Composition
Printed and bound Smythe-sewn by Arcata Graphics/Halliday
using Sebago acid-free paper